# Handbook of The Cleveland Museum of Art

# Handbook

The Cleveland Museum of Art/1978

Copyright 1978 by The Cleveland Museum of Art

*Library of Congress Cataloging in Publication Data*
Cleveland Museum of Art.
  Handbook.

  Includes index.
  1. Art—Ohio—Cleveland. 2. Cleveland Museum of Art.
N552.A6 1977    708'.171'32    76-54618
ISBN 0-910386-31-5

# Contents

# Ground Floor

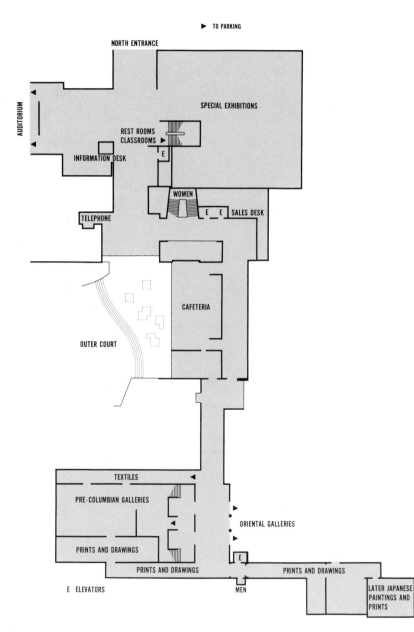

► TO PARKING

NORTH ENTRANCE

AUDITORIUM

SPECIAL EXHIBITIONS

REST ROOMS
CLASSROOMS ►

E

INFORMATION DESK

WOMEN

E  E  SALES DESK

TELEPHONE

CAFETERIA

OUTER COURT

TEXTILES

PRE-COLUMBIAN GALLERIES

ORIENTAL GALLERIES

PRINTS AND DRAWINGS

E

PRINTS AND DRAWINGS

PRINTS AND DRAWINGS

LATER JAPANESE
PAINTINGS AND
PRINTS

E  ELEVATORS

MEN

# Gallery Floor

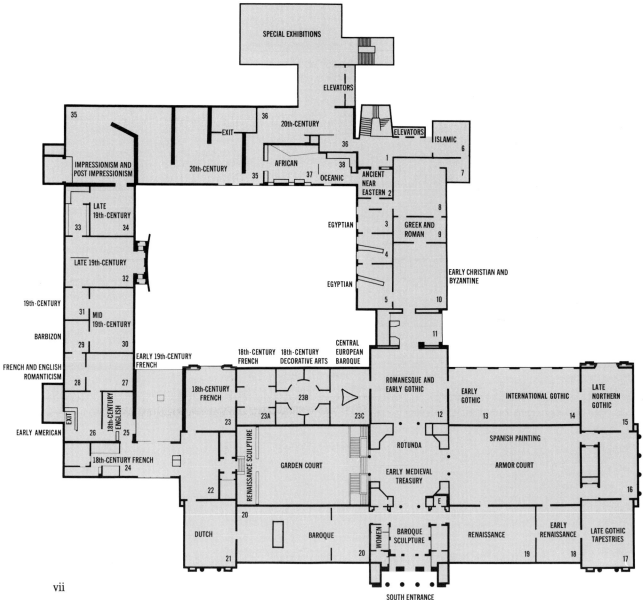

SPECIAL EXHIBITIONS

ELEVATORS

35

36

20th-CENTURY

ELEVATORS

EXIT

ISLAMIC       6

20th-CENTURY

36

1

IMPRESSIONISM AND
POST IMPRESSIONISM

AFRICAN

38

7

35

37

OCEANIC

ANCIENT
NEAR
EASTERN   2

LATE
19th-CENTURY

8

33       34

EGYPTIAN

3

GREEK AND
ROMAN

9

LATE 19th-CENTURY

4

32

EGYPTIAN

EARLY CHRISTIAN AND
BYZANTINE

19th-CENTURY

5

10

31    MID
19th-CENTURY

11

BARBIZON

29       30

FRENCH AND ENGLISH
ROMANTICISM

EARLY 19th-CENTURY
FRENCH

18th-CENTURY
FRENCH

18th-CENTURY
DECORATIVE ARTS

CENTRAL
EUROPEAN
BAROQUE

28       27

18th-CENTURY
FRENCH

23B

ROMANESQUE AND
EARLY GOTHIC

EARLY
GOTHIC

INTERNATIONAL GOTHIC

LATE
NORTHERN
GOTHIC

EXIT

18th-CENTURY
ENGLISH

23A

23C

12

13

14

15

EARLY AMERICAN

26      25

23

ROTUNDA

SPANISH PAINTING

18th-CENTURY FRENCH

24

GARDEN COURT

RENAISSANCE SCULPTURE

ARMOR COURT

22

EARLY MEDIEVAL
TREASURY

16

E

20

DUTCH

BAROQUE

WOMEN

BAROQUE
SCULPTURE

RENAISSANCE

EARLY
RENAISSANCE

LATE GOTHIC
TAPESTRIES

21

20

19       18

17

SOUTH ENTRANCE

# General Information

## Museum Hours

*Admission is free.*

Closed Monday.
Tuesday 10:00 am to 6:00 pm.
Wednesday 10:00 am to 10:00 pm.
Thursday 10:00 am to 6:00 pm.
Friday 10:00 am to 6:00 pm; for special events
  the Education Wing remains open until
  10:00 pm.
Saturday 9:00 am to 5:00 pm.
Sunday 1:00 to 6:00 pm.
Closed New Year's Day, July 4, Thanksgiving,
  and Christmas.

## Restaurant

*Luncheon:* Noon to 2:15 pm Tuesday through
  Friday and 11:45 am to 2:15 pm on Saturday.

*Afternoon tea:* 3:15 to 4:45 pm Tuesday
  through Friday and 3:00 to 4:30 pm on
  Saturday.

## Location

The Museum is located in Cleveland's University Circle area at 11150 East Boulevard. Telephone number is (216) 421-7340. The University Circle shuttle bus provides service between the Museum and nearby metropolitan rapid transit train and bus stops. Visitors' parking is adjacent to the Museum's North Entrance.

## Library

The Library is open to Museum members, visiting curators, faculty, and graduate students. Visitors are requested to show membership or university identification cards. Books, magazines, and photographs are for reference and do not circulate. Slides may be rented for educational use. The Slide Collection is open Tuesday through Saturday and the Photograph Collection Tuesday through Friday.

*Hours*

Closed Monday
Tuesday–Friday 10:00 am-5:40 pm
Saturday 9:00 am-4:40 pm
Sunday 1:00-5:40 pm when Case Western
  Reserve University is in session
Memorial Day through Labor Day:
  Tuesday–Friday 10:00 am-4:40 pm

## Sales Desk

Catalogs, color prints, post cards, Christmas cards, CMA *Bulletins,* books, slides, posters, and framed reproductions are for sale at the desk near the restaurant. A list will be mailed on request.

# Foreword

The Cleveland Museum of Art is primarily a museum devoted to the arts
of all cultures, though it differentiates itself from historical, archaeological,
and anthropological museums in an emphasis on the aesthetic quality of an
object rather than on its purely historical or documentary value. Its origins
and development present an encouraging instance of private philanthropy for
the public good.

Wade Park was given to the city of Cleveland in 1882 by the first Jeptha H.
Wade; an oval-shaped area facing the lagoon in the park was, however, reserv-
ed by the donor and passed on to his grandson, J. H. Wade II. In 1892 this
area was set aside for the erection of "a building devoted to Art and establishing therein a Museum and Gallery of Art . . . for the benefit of all the
people forever. . . ." The Cleveland Museum of Art was eventually erected on
this land.

Funds for such an institution were bequeathed by Hinman B. Hurlbut in
1881, John Huntington in 1889, and Horace Kelley in 1890, each probably
acting without the knowledge of the others. Nothing was done until in 1913
the trustees of the two latter funds cooperated to incorporate The Cleveland
Museum of Art, endowed by the Hinman B. Hurlbut Fund, with the building
cost financed by The John Huntington Art and Polytechnic Trust and The
Horace Kelley Art Foundation. The new museum was formally opened to the
public on June 6, 1916, in the classical-style building designed by the architects Hubbell and Benes and the architectural consultant Edmund B.
Wheelwright of Boston. The Museum has always been a private institution for
the public benefit, and The John Huntington Art and Polytechnic Trust and
The Horace Kelley Art Foundation have made annual grants from the begin-
ning. These funds have been augmented by bequests, grants, and membership
support, all combining to produce a sound financial foundation for the various operations of an art museum.

Soon after the Museum's opening, the first of many bequests was made:
Dudley P. Allen, a founding trustee, left a purchase fund in 1915, and the

following year Mary Warden Harkness bequeathed a fund in memory of Charles W. Harkness, as well as porcelains and paintings. Worcester R. Warner gave money to begin a collection of Oriental art. And at the time of the opening of the Museum the Severance collection of arms and armor, the tapestries given in memory of Dudley P. Allen, and, a short time later, the J. H. Wade II collection of paintings formed the basis of a continuing tradition of giving. In 1920 J. H. Wade II established a large trust fund, whose income made it possible for the Museum to purchase works of art for every department. And since 1919 our Department of Prints and Drawings has enjoyed the generous support of The Print Club of Cleveland.

Mr. and Mrs. Ralph T. King, Mrs. Leonard C. Hanna, William G. Mather, D. Z. Norton, Francis F. Prentiss, John L. Severance, Edward L. Whittemore, Mrs. Edward B. Greene, Mrs. R. Henry Norweb, and others made possible the purchase of outstanding works of art. John L. Severance and Mrs. Francis F. Prentiss began the formation of collections destined to be among the greatest bequests ever received by the Museum. In 1940 came the bequest of James Parmelee, and in 1942 the bequest of Julia Morgan Marlatt established the substantial Mr. and Mrs. William H. Marlatt Fund, the income to be used for the purchase of paintings. That year the important John L. Severance Fund was established for art acquisitions. It was also in 1942 that the first of many gifts from the Hanna Fund was received, enabling the Museum to purchase great works of art in every field. Two years later Elisabeth Severance Prentiss left her beautiful collection, together with a substantial unrestricted fund, to the Museum. In late 1957 the magnificent bequest of Leonard C. Hanna, Jr., including his art collection, established large funds for purchase and operating expenses. A complete catalogue of Mr. Hanna's many gifts was published in 1958. Among more recent examples of this continuing philanthropy are the bequest of Martha Holden Jennings, establishing a major fund for the purchase of works of art as well as for operating expenses; The Ernest L. and Louise M. Gartner Fund for the Museum's Department of Musical Arts; and The Severance and Greta Millikin Purchase Fund.

It is impossible to mention here all of the other munificent gifts recorded from time to time in the pages of *The Bulletin of The Cleveland Museum of Art,* published continuously since 1914, two years before the opening of the Museum. The growth of the collections, thanks to these generous gifts of numerous donors and to the purchases made possible by the various funds, made necessary the building of additional galleries; an additional wing, designed by Hays and Ruth, architects, was dedicated in March of 1958.

The educational activities of the Museum have matched the growth and merit of the collections. The Art History and Education Department was one of a very few pioneers in the field of children's art education, a peculiarly American development. The programs now range from those for four-year-old children to adult education and undergraduate and graduate studies in cooperation with Case Western Reserve University. The Museum's growing publications program is another aspect of this educational activity.

Educational activities increased and diversified to such an extent that it became inevitable that new quarters and facilities were necessary to accommodate them. Several special exhibition areas, a larger and more flexible auditorium, classrooms ranging in size from lecture and recital halls capable of seating more than one hundred to seminar rooms for about fifteen students, as well as offices were all part of the concept of a new education wing added to the Museum in 1971.

Because of the singular nature of the addition, the services of one of the world's leading architects was sought. Marcel Breuer and Associates designed an extremely handsome and functional building, tying it into the original structure and the wing completed in 1958 by the simple and ingenious plan of wrapping it around the facade of the later wing. Thus, the new building is integrated with the existing structures and exhibition areas, yet also can function independently when necessary to accommodate special activities. It has enabled the Museum to develop its educational program more efficiently and with greater variety than ever before.

This *Handbook* of the collections is intended to aid the visitor before and after his visits to the Museum—before, as a broad visual introduction to the wealth of material and its particular strengths; after, as a reminder of what has been seen, or missed. The arrangement of the *Handbook* is based on the historical and cultural arrangement of the galleries, finally achieved in 1977 after seven years of work.

The *Handbook* is the result of the concerted efforts of the various curatorial departments. Particular mention should be made of Rémy Saisselin, who was initially in charge of the project, and of Merald E. Wrolstad, Editor of Publications, who succeeded him and, assisted by Sally W. Goodfellow, brought the book to successful completion. Thanks are due to the Museum photographer, Nicholas C. Hlobeczy.

Sherman E. Lee, *Director*

**Art Purchase Funds**

*Art Purchase Endowment Funds*

A. W. Ellenberger Sr.
James Albert and Mary Gardiner Ford
   Memorial
Leonard C. Hanna Jr. Bequest
Lawrence Hitchcock Memorial
Delia E. Holden
L. E. Holden
Andrew R. and Martha Holden Jennings
Mr. and Mrs. William H. Marlatt
Mary Spedding Milliken Memorial
Severance and Greta Millikin
James Parmelee
Cornelia Blakemore Warner
Edward L. Whittemore

*Art Purchase Trust Funds*

Dudley P. Allen
John L. Severance
Norman O. Stone and Ella A. Stone
   Memorial
J. H. Wade

**Membership**

Annual Members contribute annually $15.
Sustaining Members contribute annually $35.
Fellows contribute annually $100.
Life Members contribute $250.
Special Life Members contribute $500.
Fellows for Life contribute $1,000.
Fellows in Perpetuity contribute $5,000.
Endowment Fellows contribute $10,000.
Benefactors contribute $25,000.
Endowment Benefactors contribute $100,000.
Benefactor Fellows contribute $250,000.
Foundation Benefactors contribute $500,000.
Endowment funds may be established with an
   initial contribution of any sum over $500.
Corporate memberships and contributions are
   encouraged and welcomed.
For further information contact the office of
   the General Manager.

*Full particulars may be had upon request.*

# Publications

Since 1916 the Museum has sponsored the publication of many studies originating in its own collections and in special exhibitions. For the past several decades it has issued a distinguished series of publications under its own imprint. World-wide distribution is arranged through a cooperative publishing program with Indiana University Press. A complete list of all CMA publications is available on request from the Museum Sales Desk.

## Catalogs of the Collection

The Museum has undertaken a publishing program which will eventually include definitive catalogs covering the entire Museum collection. Part One of the series on painting has been published:

*European Paintings before 1500* by Wolfgang Stechow, Elizabeth de Fernandez-Gimenez, Ann Tzeutschler Lurie, and Nancy Coe Wixom. xvi + 183 pages, 8-½ x 11 inches, 206 illustrations (28 color), 1974. LC: 72-83626. ISBN: 0-910386.

Part Two—*European Paintings of the Sixteenth, Seventeenth, and Eighteenth Centuries* is scheduled for publication in late 1979. Other catalogs in the CMA series currently in preparation are: *Egyptian Art in The Cleveland Museum of Art* by John D. Cooney and *Medieval Textiles in Cleveland (Part One: The Near East)* by Dorothy G. Shepherd.

## Other titles related to the Museum collection

*Selected Works: The Cleveland Museum of Art* by the Museum staff. Includes full-page illustrations of some of the most important objects in the Museum collection. x + 240 pages, 9-½ x 11-½ inches, 239 illustrations (32 color), 1967. LC: 66-21226. ISBN: 0-910386-12-9.

*Introduction to The Cleveland Museum of Art* by the Museum staff. Full-page color illustrations of key objects in the Museum collection are accompanied by text written by the departmental curator. 104 pages, 7 x 7 inches, 48 color illustrations, 1975. ISBN: 3-7821-2113-9.

*The First Fifty Years: The Cleveland Museum of Art, 1916-1966* by Carl Wittke. An accomplished social historian's account of the Museum's history. xiv + 162 pages, 6 x 9 inches, illustrated, 1966. LC: 66-21227. ISBN: 0-910386-09-09.

*Rodin Sculpture in The Cleveland Museum of Art* by Athena Tacha Spear. x + 102 pages, 7-½ x 9 inches, 114 illustrations, 1967. ISBN: 0-910386-11-0. *Supplement* (1974), vi + 34 pages, 7-½ x 9 inches, 27 illustrations. LC: 67-28952. ISBN: 0-910386-20-x.

*African Tribal Images: The Katherine White Reswick Collection* by William Fagg. xxii + 238 pages, 8-¾ x 9-¼ inches, 380 illustrations and map, 1968. ISBN: 0-910386-15-3.

*Fabergé and His Contemporaries: The India Early Minshall Collection of The Cleveland Museum of Art* by Henry Hawley. A stunning collection of the *objets de vertu* created by the Russian court jeweler Carl Fabergé and his firm. vi + 139 pages, 7-½ x 9 inches, 63 illustrations (8 color), 1967. ISBN: 0-910386-10-2.

*Renaissance Bronzes from Ohio Collections* by William D. Wixom. Includes over 230 bronzes from the collections of the Cleveland Museum, the Toledo Museum of Art, the Allen Memorial Art Museum at Oberlin College, and a number of private collectors. x + 184 pages, 8-¾ x 9-¼ inches, 276 illustrations (6 color), 1975. LC: 75-30966. ISBN: 0-910386-24-2.

*Traditions and Revisions: Themes from the History of Sculpture* by Gabriel P. Weisberg with with an introduction by H. W. Janson. A fresh approach to sculpture illustrated with over 100 works from the Museum collection. x + 144 pages, 8-¼ x 10-½ inches, 119 illustrations (2 color), 1975. LC: 75-26705. ISBN: 0-910386-23-4.

*The Bulletin of The Cleveland Museum of Art* is a scholarly periodical published ten times a year. Its range of subjects is as wide as the Museum's interests—which means that an issue can contain a discussion of a school of Chinese ceramics, a medieval crucifix, or an abstract sculpture, or all three. Published monthly except July and August. 7-½ x 9 inches, illustrated, about 300 pages a year. Subscriptions: $10.00 per year ($8.00 for Museum members); $1.00 per copy.

THEMES IN ART is a series of low-priced books about art, art history, and artistic expression written by staff members of the Department of Art History and Education. Designed with an easy-to-read format, each book is amply illustrated—not only with works from the Cleveland Museum but also from other sources. Three or four books are planned each year. Titles already published include:

*Materials and Techniques of
  20th-Century Artists*
*In the Nature of Materials:
  Japanese Decorative Arts*
*Between Past and Present: French, English,
  and American Etching 1850-1950*
*A Study in Regional Taste:
  The May Show 1919-1975*
*The Public Monument and Its Audience*
*The Artist and the Studio in the Eighteenth
  and Nineteenth Centuries*
*American Folk Art from the Traditional
  to the Naive*

# Ancient Near Eastern Art

2

*Gudea, Ensi of Lagash.* Dolerite.
Mesopotamia, Neo-Sumerian
Period, 22nd century BC.
H. 122.2 cm.  63.154

*Hittite Priest-King Figure.*
Basalt, North Syria, ca. 1600 BC.
H. 87.6 cm.  71.45

*Silver Cup with Hunting Scene.* Repoussé and engraved.
Northwestern Iran (Amlash?), end of 2nd millennium BC.
D. 16.6 cm.  65.25

*Recumbent Bull.* Fine-grained black stone, basalt (?)
Mesopotamia, Sumerian, ca. 2700 BC. L. 13.6 cm.  70.61

3

*Winged Genie.* Relief from the palace of Ashur-Nasirapal II at Nimrud. Gypseous alabaster. Mesopotamia, Assyrian Period, 885-860 BC. H. 248.9 cm. 43.246

*Plaque: Man and Griffin.* Ivory. Syria, Phoenician, 9th-8th century BC. H. 6.5 cm. 68.45

*Crouching Woman.* Ivory. Syria, Phoenician, 9th-8th century BC. H. 3.5 cm. 64.426

*Votive Pin* (detail). Silver, repoussé and engraved. Iran, Luristan, ca. 1000 BC. D. 16 cm. 63.257

*The Bear Lady.* Terra cotta. Northwestern Iran, Marlik, ca. 1000 BC. H. 21.4 cm. 67.35

4

*Gold Beaker.* Repoussé and engraved. Northwestern Iran, Marlik (?), end of 2nd millennium BC. H. 14 cm. 65.26

*Cheek Plaque of Horse Bit.* Bronze, cast and engraved. Iran, Luristan, ca. 1200-1000 BC. H. 14.9 cm. 61.33

*Finial in Form of Ibex Protome.* Cast bronze. Iran, Luristan, late 7th century BC. H. 22.3 cm. 65.554

*Beaker.* Silver, repoussé and engraved. Iran, Luristan, 8th-7th century BC. H. 10.2 cm. 63.95

*Ibex Head Finial.* Cast bronze. Iran,
Achaemenid Period, 6th-5th century
BC. H. 17.2 cm. 61.199

*Bull's Head.* Cast bronze. Iran,
Urartu, 8th-7th century BC.
H. 15.9 cm. 42.204

*Rhyton in Form of Ram's Head.* Silver, repoussé and engraved. Iran, Kaplantu,
Median Period, 7th century BC. L. 30.5 cm. 63.479

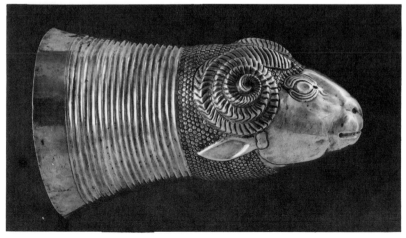

*Incense Burner.* Cast bronze. Iran, Parthian Period.
1st century. H. 11.5 cm. 61.32

*Rhyton: The Angel Drvaspa.* Silver,
repoussé, chased, and partially
gilt. Soghdia, Hephtalite Period,
5th-6th century. H. 19 cm. 64.96

*Relief Plaque with Royal Hunting
Scene: Ardashir II (?) Hunting Lions.*
Alabaster. Iran, Sasanian Period,
late 4th century. D. 49 cm. 63.258

*Ibex Relief.* Carved stucco. Iran,
Sasanian Period, 6th century.
H. 30.8 cm. 41.24

*Plate with Royal Hunting Scene: King Hormizd Hunting Lions.* Silver, applied cast relief, chased, engraved, and partially gilt. Iran, Sasanian Period, reign of Hormizd II (AD 302-309). D. 20.6 cm. 62.150

*Wine Vessel: Figures of the Goddess Anahita.* Silver, cast, engraved, and partially gilt. Iran, Sasanian Period, early 4th century. H. 18.5 cm. 62.294

*Plate: The Goddess Anahita.* Silver, applied cast relief, chased, engraved, and partially gilt. Iran, Sasanian Period, early 4th century. D. 21.6 cm. 62.295

*Rhyton in Form of a Horse.* Silver, repoussé, engraved, and gold overlay. Iran, Sasanian Period, 4th century. H. 21 cm. 64.41

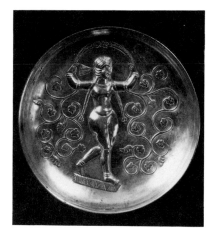

8

*Textile.* Compound twill weave, silk. Iran, Sasanian
Period, 6th-7th century. W. 11.4 cm. 51.88

*Textile.* Tapestry weave, wool and linen. Iran,
Sasanian Period, late 6th-early 7th century.
W. 24.8 cm. 50.509

*Notes*

# Egyptian Art

12

*Ny-kau-re, Overseer of the Granary.*
Red granite. Sakkara, 2nd half of
Dynasty V, ca. 2400-2345 BC.
H. 54 cm.  64.90

*Panel from False Door of Ny-kau-re.*
Limestone. Sakkara, 2nd half of
Dynasty V, ca. 2400-2345 BC.
H. 116.9 cm.  64.91

*Statue of Heqat.* Alabaster.
Dynasty I, ca. 3100 BC. H. 15.6 cm.
76.5

*Relief from the Tomb of Ankh-ni-nesut.* Limestone. Sakkara, Dynasty VI,
ca. 2200 BC. W. 174 cm.  30.736

13

*Amenemhet III.* Black granite.
Karnak, late Dynasty XII, ca.
1800 BC. H. 50.5 cm. 60.56

*Family Tomb Stela of Four Persons.*
Limestone. First Intermediate
Period, ca. 2150 BC. W. 75 cm.
14.543

*Four Nome Gods Bearing Offerings below Fragmentary Scene of Amenhotep III before the God Amun.* Painted limestone
relief. Thebes, funerary temple of Amenhotep III, Dynasty XVIII, ca. 1390 BC. Entire width 131.5 cm. 61.205, 76.51

*Head of Queen Hatshepsut.* Green schist. Thebes, Dynasty XVIII, ca. 1490 BC. H. 16.2 cm. 17.976

*Coronation Portrait of Amenhotep III.* Gray granite. Thebes, Dynasty XVIII, early reign of Amenhotep III, ca. 1417 BC. H. 39.4 cm. 52.513

*Head of Amenhotep III.* Brown quartzite. Dynasty XVIII, late reign of Amenhotep III, ca. 1380 BC. H. 16 cm. 61.417

*Seated Cat.* Black hematite. Late Dynasty XVIII(?), ca. 1355 BC. H. 4.4 cm. 73.29

*King's Scribe Amenhotep and His Wife Renut.* Limestone relief. Assiut, Deir el Durunka, Dynasty XIX, early reign of Ramesses II, ca. 1290 BC. W. 123 cm. 63.100

15

*Queen Nefertiti.* Sandstone sunk
relief. Karnak, Dynasty XVIII,
early reign of Amenhotep IV,
1379-1374 BC. W. 28 cm. 59.188

*Nefertiti Offering to the Aten.* Sandstone sunk relief. Karnak, pillar
courtyard(?), Dynasty XVIII, early reign of Amenhotep IV, 1379-1374 BC.
W. 43.5 cm. 59.186

*Queen Nefertiti.* Sandstone sunk
relief, heavily painted. Karnak,
Dynasty XVIII, early reign of
Amenhotep IV, 1379-1374 BC.
W. 27 cm. 76.4

*Coffin of Bekenmut* (detail).
Painting on gesso over wood.
Probably from Thebes, Dynasty XXII,
ca. 900 BC. H. of coffin 208. 3 cm.
14.561

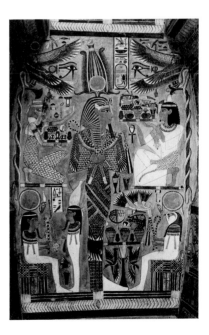

*Birds Among Papyrus* (relief from Tomb of Mentuemhat).
Limestone. Thebes, early Dynasty XXVI, ca. 660 BC.
W. 41.6 cm. 49.498

*Mentuemhat in Ecclesiastical Dress*
(relief from his tomb). Limestone.
Thebes, early Dynasty XXVI, ca.
660 BC. H. 103.6 cm. 51.280

*Offering Bearers* (relief from Tomb of Mentuemhat). Limestone. Thebes,
early Dynasty XXVI, ca. 660 BC. W. 58.4 cm. 51.284

*Horwedja Presenting a Statue to
His God.* Black schist. Dynasty
XXVII, ca. 500 BC. H. 43.7 cm.
20.1978

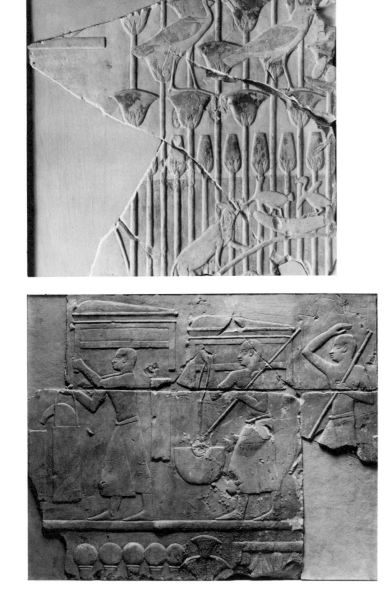

*Stela of Djed-atum-iuf-ankh.* Yellow crystalline quartzite. Heliopolis, Dynasty XXV, ca. 700 BC., imitating style of Old Kingdom. H. 28 cm. 20.1977

*Mongoose.* Bronze. Ca. 600 BC or later. L. 21 cm. 64.358

*Female Musicians* (fragment of a lintel joining another fragment now in Berlin). Limestone relief. Lower Egyptian School, Dynasty XXX, ca. 350 BC. W. 33 cm. 14.542

*Torso of the General Amen-pe-Yom.* Gray granite. Temple at Mendes, early 3rd century BC. H. 95.3 cm. 48.141

18

*Funerary Portrait of a Young Girl.*
Encaustic painting and gilt on wood
panel. Hawara, 2nd century AD.
H. 40 cm.  71.137

*Funerary Portrait of a Woman.*
Encaustic painting on linen.
Faiyum, ca. 1st century AD.
H. 24.7 cm.  71.136

*Notes*

# Classical Art

22

*Kouros Torso.* Island marble. Greece, ca. 560-540 BC. H. 62.6 cm. 53.125

*Mirror* (detail). Bronze. Greece, ca. 470-460 BC. Overall H. 38.8 cm. 50.7

*Black-Figured Nikosthenes Amphora* (signed by potter). Painted terra cotta. Greece, Attic, ca. 540-530 BC. H. 31.1 cm. 74.10

*Red-Figured Eye Kylix by Psiax.* Painted terra cotta. Greece, ca. 520 BC. D. 34.3 cm. 76.89

23

*Athlete as a Mirror Support.* Bronze. South Italy, Locri, provincial Greek, 460-450 BC. H. 22.5 cm. 28.659

*Standing Athlete.* Bronze. Greece, Attic, School of Polykleitos, ca. 460 BC. H. 19.7 cm. 55.685

*Statuette of a Rider.* Bronze, Greece, ca. 440 BC. H. 13.4 cm. 77.41

*Black-Figured Hydria by the Antimenes Painter.* Painted terra cotta. Greek, Attic, ca. 525 BC. H. 43.2 cm. 75.1

*The Cleveland Krater.* Red-figured terra cotta, Greece, Attic, early 5th century BC. H. 56.5 cm. 30.104

*Atalanta Lekythos by Douris.* White-ground terra cotta. Greece, 500-490 BC. H. 31.8 cm. 66.114

24

*Charging Bull.* Bronze. Greece, Lucania, late 5th century BC. L. 18.5 cm. 30.336

*Head of the God Pan.* Painted limestone. Greece, Attic, ca. 490 BC. H. 35 cm. 26.538

*Grave Monument.* Marble. Greece, Attic, ca. 400-350 BC. H. 128.3 cm. 24.1018

*Head of a Lion.* Terra cotta. Italy, provincial Greek, 5th century BC. H. 11.8 cm. 27.27

*Mirror Rest: Siren.* Bronze inlaid with silver. Greece, Corinth, ca. 475 BC. H. 11.5 cm. 67.204

*Torso of a Youth.* Marble. Greece, ca. 150-100 BC. H. 103.2 cm. 65.23

*Dancing Lady.* Mainland (Peloponnesus) marble. Greece, Alexandria(?), eclectic work, ca. 50-25 BC. H. 85.5 cm. 65.24

*Head of a Barbarian.* Marble. Greece, School of Pergamon, late 3rd century BC. H. 10.5 cm. 29.440

*Mirror Case with Head of Athena.* Bronze. Greece, ca. 385 BC. D. 11.3 cm. 72.66,a

*Perfume Container in Form of an Askos* (skin). Agate, with gold mounts. East Greek, Amisos (Turkey), ca. 2nd century BC or later(?). H. 6.5 cm. 64.92

*Skyphos.* Silver. Greece, 3rd century BC. D. 15.3 cm. 77.166

*Standing Warrior.* Bronze. Italy,
Rimini(?), Etruscan, ca. 500-450
BC. H. 28 cm.  67.32

*Cista Handle: The Genii Sleep and Death Carrying off
Fallen Memnon.* Bronze. Italy, Etruscan, 2nd half 4th
century BC. W. 17.5 cm.  45.13

*Satyr Finial from a Kottabos Stand.*
Bronze. Italy, Etruscan, ca. 470
BC. H. 15 cm.  74.16

*Incense Burner Supported by
Youthful Dionysus.* Bronze. Italy,
Etruscan, 2nd century BC.
H. 61 cm.  52.96

27

*Duck-Askos.* Painted terra cotta. Italy, Etruscan, 4th
century BC. L. 25 cm. 75.23

*Furniture Ornament: Head of a Mule.*
Bronze. Russia (Kertch),
Hellenistic, ca. 1st century BC-
1st century AD. H. 20.4 cm. 43.68

*Hair Ringlets.* Gold. Sicily, Hellenistic, ca. 4th
century BC. W. 3.5 cm. and 3.2 cm. 68.102-.103

*Standing Harpocrates.* Bronze,
inlaid with silver. Egypt,
Alexandria, ca. 1st century BC.
H. 27 cm. 72.6

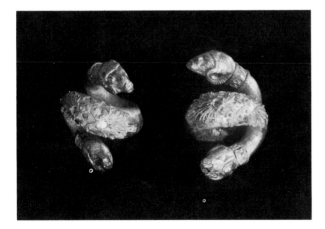

28

*Head of a Man (C. Cornelius Gallus?).* Marble. Egypt, ca. 30 BC. H. 32.8 cm. 66.20

*Portrait Bust of a Man.* Bronze. Roman, Late Republican, 40-30 BC. H. 38.1 cm. 28.860

*Negro Beggar.* Bronze, with silver and copper inlays. Egypt, Alexandria, 2nd-1st century BC. H. 18.6 cm. 63.507

*Vicarello Goblet.* Silver. Italy, Vicarello, Roman, late 1st century BC-early 1st century AD. H. 11.2 cm. 66.371

*Oil Ampulla in the Form of a Dancing Bear.* Bronze. Italy(?), Roman, 3rd century AD. H. 14.6 cm. 72.102

*Portrait Head of a Man.* Marble.
Roman, ca. AD 100. H. 27 cm.
25.944

*The Co-Emperor Lucius Verus.*
Crystalline island marble.
Provincial Roman, from Alexandria,
ca. AD 170-180. H. 38.1 cm. 52.260

*Apollo and Nike.* Marble relief. Roman, Neo-Attic School,
late 1st century BC-early 1st century AD. W. 46.4 cm.
30.522

*Torso of Apollo.* Marble. Roman,
early 2nd century AD(?).
H. 87.7 cm. 24.1017

*Head of the Emperor Balbinus.*
Marble. Roman, ca. AD 238.
H. 18.5 cm.  25.945

*Tomb Relief.* Crystalline limestone. Syria, Palmyra, ca. AD 230.
W. 73.7 cm.  64.359

*The Alexander Plate.* Gold-glass.
Italy, Roman, AD 235. D. 25.7 cm.
69.68

*Procession of Nobles.* Limestone relief. Syria, Palmyra, AD 100-150.
L. 120.7 cm.  70.15

# Notes

# Early Christian and Byzantine Art

*Spoon.* Silver with partial gilding
and niello inscription. Byzantium,
mid-4th century. L. 12.5 cm.
64.39

*Bowl.* Silver. Byzantium, Syria (?), 4th century.
D. 27.8 cm. 54.259

*The Good Shepherd and Jonah Under the Gourd Vine: Two of a Group of Sculptures.* Marble. Eastern Mediterranean,
end of the 3rd quarter of the 3rd century. H. 50.2 and 32.1 cm. 65.241, 65.239

35

*Lamp and Stand.* Silver. Byzantium, Syria (?), late 4th century. H. 48.9 cm.  54.597

*Lunette.* Limestone. Egypt, Coptic Period, 5th century. W. 61 cm.  55.63

*Lamp for Suspension with Griffin Head and Christian Monograms.* Bronze. Byzantium, 4th-5th century. H. 14.5 cm.  74.77

*Bowl.* Silver with niello. Byzantium, Syria (?), second half 4th century. D. 18.5 cm.  56.30

*Bust of an Empress.* Byzantium, Theodosian Period, late 4th century. H. 10.2 cm.  67.28

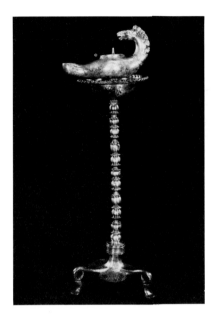

36

*Maenad and Satyr.* Tapestry weave, wool and linen. Egypt, Late Roman or Early Byzantine Period, 2nd–4th century. H. 138 cm. 75.6

*The Nereid.* Tapestry weave, wool and linen. Egypt, Byzantine Period, late 4th–early 5th century. H. 66.5 cm. 53.18

*Textile.* Tapestry weave, wool and linen. Egypt, Byzantine Period, 5th century. H. 20.5 cm. 16.1980

*Dancing Pan.* Limestone. Egypt, Coptic Period, 4th-5th century. H. 34 cm. 55.68

*Icon of the Virgin.* Tapestry, wool. Egypt, Byzantine Period, 6th century. H. 179.5 cm. 67.144

37

*The Piping Maenad.* Fragment of a
hanging. Loop knot pile, wool and
linen. Egypt, Byzantine Period,
6th century. H. 83.5 cm. 68.74

*Textile.* Tapestry weave, wool and
linen. Egypt, Antinoë, Byzantine
Period, 6th century. H. 76 cm.
60.273

*Textile.* Tapestry weave, wool.
Egypt, Antinoë, Byzantine Period,
6th century. H. 43 cm. 48.27

*Textile:* Tapestry weave, wool. Egypt, Antinoë,
Byzantine Period, 6th century. Over-all: W. 158 cm.
Detail: H. 26.7 cm. 61.201

37

*Vase.* Silver with gilding.
Byzantium, Syria(?), late 4th-
6th century. H. 39.7 cm. 57.497

*Chalice Dedicated to St. Sergius.*
Silver. Byzantium, Syria, 6th-7th
century. H. 17.4 cm. 50.378

*Pyx.* Ivory. Byzantium, 6th century.
H. 8.4 cm. 51.114

*Sarcophogus Relief.* From S. Carlino, Ravenna. Marble. Byzantium,
Ravenna, early 6th century. H. 99.7 cm. 48.25

39

*Portrait Intaglio.* Garnet, gold
filigree. Byzantium, 6th century.
H. 3.3 cm. 47.33

*Paten Dedicated to St. Sergius.*
Silver. Possibly from Benmisonas,
Syria. Byzantium, 6th century.
D. 32.2 cm. 50.381

*Chain with Pendant and Two Crosses.*
Gold with enamel and glass.
Byzantium, probably Syria, early
6th century. L. of chain 31.5 cm.
47.35

*Textile: Scenes from the Old and
New Testaments.* Resist-dyed linen.
Egypt, Byzantine Period, 6th
century. Over-all: H. 104 cm.
Detail: H. 61 cm. 51.400

*Necklace with Pendants.* Gold, two
garnets. Byzantium, 6th century.
L. of chain 55.9 cm. 54.3

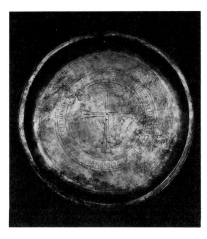

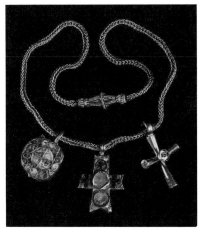

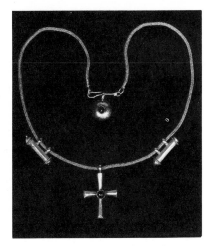

*Necklace with Pendants.* Gold with garnet.
Byzantium, 6th century. L. of chain 45.7 cm. 46.260

*Rouge Pot.* Glass, sapphire, gold
filigree. Byzantium, 6th century.
H. 3.7 cm. 46.427

*Monogram of Christ (Chrismon).*
Gold with garnets. Byzantium,
Syria, 6th-7th century. H. 15 cm.
65.551

*Textile: The Falconer.* Tapestry
weave, wool. Egypt, Umayyad Period,
second half 7th century. H. 7.5 cm.
41.293

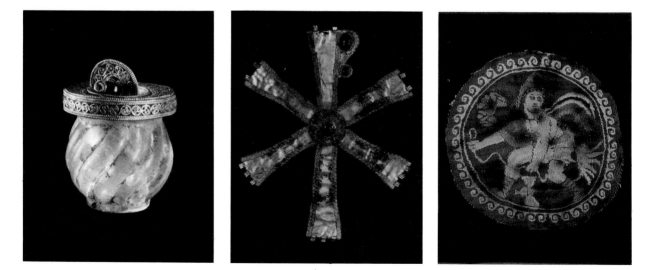

41

*Textile.* Tapestry weave, wool and linen. Egypt, Late Byzantine—Early
Umayyad Period, 7th century. Over-all: W. 22.8 cm. Detail: H. 8.3 cm.
60.275

*Embroidery: St. George.* Silk on
linen. Egypt, Tulunid Period, 9th
century. H. 10 cm. 48.115

*Textile.* Compound twill weave,
silk. Egypt, Umayyad Period, early
8th century. W. 22.8 cm. 47.192

42

*Medallion: Bust of Christ.* Steatite. Byzantium, late 9th-10th century. D. 4.1 cm. 47.37

*St. George of Cappadocia.* Quartz (variety bloodstone). Byzantium, 10th century. H. 3 cm. 59.41

*Pendant.* From the treasury of Aachen. 1) Relief: *Madonna and Child.* Steatite. Byzantium, 10th century. 2) Frame. Gilt silver and pearls. Germany, Aachen, mid-14th century. H. 6.9 cm. 51.445

*Page from a Gospel Book: St. Matthew.* Tempera and gold leaf on vellum. Byzantium, Constantinople, 1057-1063. H. 28.6 cm. 42.1512

*Single Leaf from the Epistles in a Manuscript (Pantokrator Ms. 49): St. Peter.* Tempera and gold leaf on vellum. Byzantium, Constantinople, 11th century. H. 29.4 cm. 50.154

*Greek Gospels with Commentaries.* Parchment, tempera, and gold leaf. Byzantium, 11th century. H. 29.4 cm. 42.152

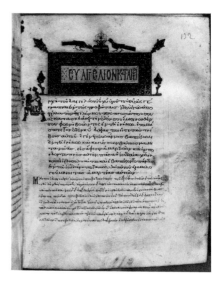

43

*Casket with Adam and Eve.* Ivory plaques over wood. Byzantium, 11th-12th century. L. 46.7 cm. 24.747

*Pyx with Christ, the Twelve Apostles and the Virgin Orans.* Ivory. Byzantium, "Triptych Group," late 10th-early 11th century. H. 9.5 cm. 73.4

*Madonna and Child Enthroned with Angels.* Ivory. Byzantium, 11th century. H. 25.4 cm. 25.1293

*Pendant Icon.* Repoussé silver gilt, cloisonné enamel. Byzantium, probably Constantinople, 11th century. H. 5.1 cm. 72.94

44

*Textile: Basilisk Motive.* Compound twill weave, silk. Byzantium, ca. 12th century. H. 34.5 cm. 74.99

*Scenes from a Passion Cycle of Christ.* Steatite relief. Byzantium, 11th-12th century. H. 11.8 cm. 62.27

*Deep Plate with Hawk and Foliage.* Sgraffito earthenware. Byzantium, mid-12th century. D. 22.2 cm. 67.139

*Notes*

# The Western Tradition

48

*Medallion with the Bust of Christ.*
From the Guelph Treasure. Cloisonné
enamel on copper. Frankish, second
half 8th century. D. 4.9 cm. 30.504

*Fibula.* Silver gilt with garnets.
Ostrogothic, early 6th century.
L. 13.3 cm. 75.108

*Crossbow Fibula.* Bronze. Gallo-
Roman, late 4th-5th century.
L. 10.2 cm. 30.227

*Group of Ornaments.* Bronze and
enamel. Gallo-Roman, 2nd-3rd
century. H. from 3.8 to 6.1 cm.
30.230-30.234

*Well Head.* Limestone. Italy,
Venice (?), Langobardic, 8th-9th
century. H. 66.7 cm. 16.1982

49

*Title Page of Abbot Berno's "Tonarius."* Tempera, ink, and gold on parchment. Germany, Reichenau, ca. 1020-1030. H. 21.4 cm. 52.88

*Christ's Mission to the Apostles.* Ivory. Germany, Ottonian, ca. 970. H. 18.3 cm. 67.65

*Leaf from a Gradual and Sacramentary (Trier Codex 151).* Tempera, ink, and gold on parchment. Austria, Salzburg, early 11th century. H. 22.1 cm. 33.447

*Double Leaf from a Roman Gradual.* Gold uncials and silver rustic capitals on purple parchment. German, Lotharingia, Trier(?), last quarter 10th century. H. 28.6 cm. 33.446

50

*Reliquary in the Form of a Book.*
From the Guelph Treasure. Ivory.
Valley of the Meuse, Liége, ca. 1000.
Frame: Germany, Lower Saxony,
Brunswick, 2nd half 14th century.
H. 31.8 cm. 30.741

*Gertrudis Portable Altar; First and Second Gertrudis Crosses.* From the
Guelph Treasure. Gold, cloisonné enamel, semi-precious stones, and
porphyry. Germany, Lower Saxony, Brunswick, ca. 1040. Altar: L. 26.7 cm.;
Crosses: H. 24.2 cm. 31.462, 31.55, 31.461

*Châsse.* Champlevé enamel on copper
over oak core. France, Limousin,
Limoges, late 12th or early 13th
century. H. 17.5 cm. 54.599

*Reliquary Casket.* Boxwood. England,
Anglo-Saxon, ca. 960-980. H. 8.9 cm.
53.362

*Capitals.* From Preuilly-sur-Claise. Limestone with traces of polychromy. France, Southern Touraine, mid-12th century. H. 68 cm. 30.18

*Capital with Fantastic birds and Basilisk.* Limestone. France, Bordelais (Dordogne), 12th century. H. 53.3 cm. 68.34

*Cross.* Champlevé enamel and gilding on copper. Master of the Grandmont Altar, French, Limousin, ca. 1189. H. 67 cm. 23.1051

*Engaged Capital: Daniel in the Lion's Den.* Limestone. France, Basin of the Loire, mid-12th century. H. 73.7 cm. 62.247

*Plaque from a Châsse Showing the Crucifixion and the Martyrdom of Saint Thomas Becket.* Gilt copper, champlevé enamel. Ca. 1220-1225. Attr. to Master G. Alpais and his workshop, French, Limousin, Limoges. W. 28.4 cm. 51.449

52

*Fragment of a Capital.* Stone. South Italy, Atelier of the Cathedral of Monopoli, early 12th century. H. 36.8 cm. 55.556

*Single Page from a Decretum by Gratianus.* Tempera on parchment. France, Burgundy, Pontigny, ca. 1160-1165. H. 43.8 cm. 54.598

*Bible Miniature Showing St. Luke.* Tempera, ink, and gold on parchment. France, Burgundy, Abbey of Cluny, ca. 1100. H. 17.1 cm. 68.190

*Plaques from a Portable Altar.* Walrus ivory. Germany, Lower Rhine Valley, 2nd half 11th century. H. of each 5.1 cm. 22.307-22.309

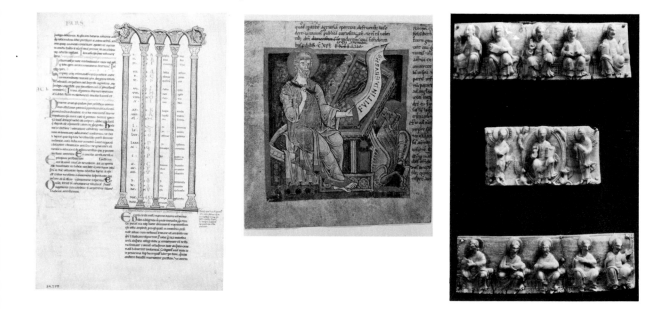

53

*Engaged Capital: Carytidal Figure
(Daniel) Flanked by Lions.* Limestone.
France, possibly Poitou, 2nd quarter
12th century. H. 34.3 cm. 63.477

*Reliquary.* Champlevé enamel and
gilding on copper. Valley of the
Meuse, ca. 1160, Circle of
Godefroid de Claire. H. 19.7 cm.
26.428

*Historiated Initial A from an
Antiphonary Tree of Jesse.* Tempera,
ink, gold, and silver on parchment.
Valley of the Meuse, ca. 1115-1125.
H. 18.7 cm. 49.202

*Corpus of Christ.* Cast bronze with
traces of gilding. Valley of the
Meuse, 3rd quarter 12th century.
H. 9.9 cm. 69.50

*Mourning Mary* (probably from Altar
Cross). Gilt bronze. Valley of the
Meuse, early 13th century.
H. 10.2 cm. 70.351

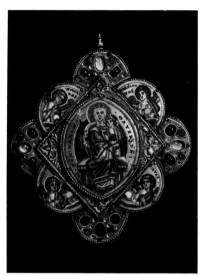

1) *Paten of St. Bernward.* From the Guelph Treasure. Gilt silver and niello. Ca. 1175. Master of the Oswald Reliquary, German, Hildesheim.
2) *Monstrance.* Gilt silver and rock crystal. Germany, Brunswick (?), end of 14th century. H. 34.3 cm. 30.505

*Hosea.* Champlevé enamel, niello and gilding on copper. Germany, Lower Saxony, ca. 1180. H. 8.9 cm. 50.577

*Reliquary in the Form of a Portable Altar.* Champlevé and cloisonné enamel on copper, over wood core. Germany, Lower Saxony, Hildesheim, ca. 1175. W. 21.3 cm. 49.431

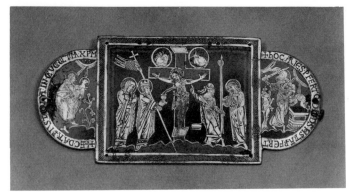

55

*Columnar Figure of an Apostle.*
From Notre-Dame-en-Vaux, Châlons-
sur-Marne. Limestone. France,
Champagne, ca. 1180. H. 97.8 cm.
19.38

*Capital.* Limestone. France,
Languedoc, 12th century. H. 34.9 cm.
16.1981

*Reliquary.* Champlevé enamel on copper over wood core.
Denmark or North Germany, 12th century. H. 9.2 cm.
49.16

56

*Arm Reliquary.* From the Guelph
Treasure. Gilt silver over oak core,
champlevé enamel. Germany, Lower
Saxony, Hildesheim, ca. 1175, by a
Follower of Eilbertus. H. 50.8 cm.
30.739

*Mourning Mary from a Crucifixion
Group.* Painted wood. Austria,
Southern Salzburg, Lungau, mid-13th
century. H. 43.8 cm.  57.500

*Leaf from a Gospel Book (now Trier
Ms. 142): Nativity (recto).* Tempera,
silver, and gold on parchment. Co-
worker of Hermann von Helmarshausen,
German, Lower Saxony, 1170-1190.
H. 34.4 cm.  33.445

*Mourning St. John from a Crucifixion
Group.* Painted wood. Austria,
Southern Salzburg, Lungau, mid-13th
century. H. 43.8 cm.  58.189

*Griffin* (one of a pair). Marble.
North Italy, ca. 1220. H. 78.1 cm.
28.861

57

*Engaged Capital: Lion and Basilisk.*
Marble. Northern Italy, late 12th
century. H. 30.2 cm. 72.20

*Title Page of "Moralia of Gregorius"*
*(now Engelberg Codex 20).* Tempera
and ink on parchment. Attr. to
Abbot Frowin, Switzerland, 1143-
1178. H. 27 cm. 55.74

*Lion Aquamanile.* Brass. Northern
Germany, Lower Saxony, probably
Hildesheim, mid-13th century.
H. 26.2 cm. 72.167

*"The Horn of St. Blasius."* From the
Guelph Treasure. Ivory. Sicily,
12th century. L. 48.9 cm. 30.740

*The Virgin from a Crucifixion Group.*
Painted and gilded wood. Spain,
Castile, ca. 1275. H. 151.1 cm.
30.622

*St. John from a Crucifixion Group.*
Painted and gilded wood. Spain,
Castile, ca. 1275. H. 154.9 cm.
30.621

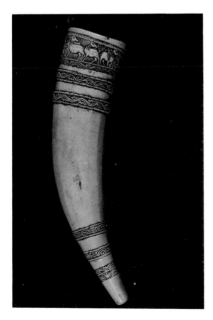

*Pair of Angels.* Walnut with traces of paint and gilding. Northeast France, probably Rheims, ca. 1235-1245. H. 73.7 and 78.7 cm. 66.360, 67.27

*Enthroned Virgin and Child.* Ivory. Valley of the Meuse, mid-13th century. H. 13.3 cm. 28.760

*Quadrilobed Plaque.* Gold with cloisonné and translucent enamel. Ca. 1300. Close to Guillaume Julien, French, Paris. H. 4.8 cm. 32.537

*Central Plaque from a Triptych: Virgin and Child with Two Angels.* Ivory. France, Paris, end of 1st third 14th century. H. 22.9 cm. 23.719

*Diptych: Scenes from the Flagellation, Crucifixion, Resurrection and Noli Me Tangere.* Ivory. France, Ile-de-France, 14th century. H. 16.8 cm. 75.110

*Madonna and Child.* Limestone with traces of paint and gilding. France, Lorraine, ca. 1310-1320. H. 75.8 cm. 74.14

*Head of an Apostle.* Limestone with traces of paint. France, Languedoc, Toulouse, 2nd quarter 14th century H. 35.6 cm. 60.170

*Angel of the Annunciation.* Marble with paint and gold leaf. France, mid-14th century. H. 56.5 cm. 54.387

*Processional Cross.* Copper gilt and champlevé enamel over wood core. Germany, Upper Rhine, Lake Constance, ca. 1280. H. 50.2 cm. 42.1091

*Aquamanile: Saddled Horse.* Bronze. Northern Germany, ca. 1300. H. 23.2 cm. 69.26

*Christ and St. John the Evangelist.* Painted wood. Germany, Swabia, near Bodensee (Lake Constance), early 14th century. H. 92.7 cm. 28.753

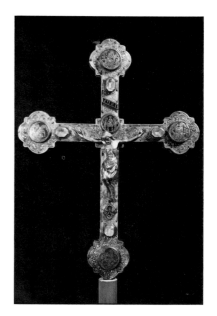

*Lenten Cloth.* Linen embroidery (white on white). Germany, Altenberg a. d. Lahn, second half 13th century. W. 393.7 cm. 48.352

*Leaf from a Gradual with Historiated Initial I with Scenes from the Life of St. Augustine.* Tempera and burnished gold leaf on parchment. The Second Master of the Wettinger Gradual, German, Lower Rhine, Cologne (?), early 14th century. H. 57.8 cm. 49.203

*Diptych: Consecretion of St. Martin of Tours* (left); *St. Martin Dividing His Cloak with a Beggar* (right). Ivory. Germany, Rhenish, second quarter 14th century. H. 9 cm. 71.103

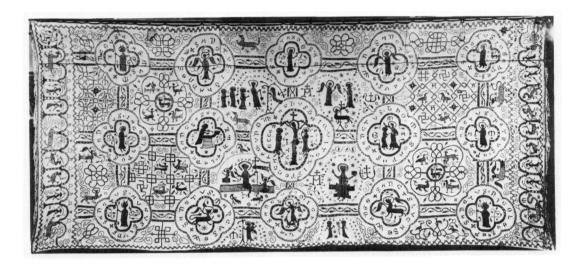

*Triptych: The Madonna and Child with Saints.* Panel. Berlinghiero (Berlinghiero di Milanese the Elder), Italian, Lucca, active ca. 1200-1240. W. 51.5 cm. 66.237

*Frontispiece Miniature of the Mariegola of the Scuola di San Giovanni Evangelista.* Tempera and gold leaf on parchment. Italy, Venice, 1st third 14th century. H. 27.3 cm. 59.128

*Initial C from Choir Book: A Pope and Assistants Celebrating Mass.* Tempera on parchment. Italy, Bologna (?), ca. 1300. H. 22.9 cm. 24.1010

*Textile.* Lampas weave, silk and gold. Italy, Lucca (?), 1st half 14th century. Over-all: H. 81.2 cm. Detail: H. 48.2 cm. 26.507

*Albarello.* Majolica. Spain, Valencia, Paterna, 14th century. H. 21.6 cm. 45.28

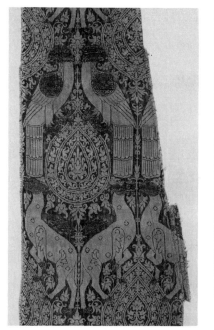

63

Polyptych: *Madonna and Child with St. Francis, St. John the Baptist, St. James the Great, and Mary Magdalen.* Panel. Ugolino di Nerio da Siena, Italian, Siena, active ca. 1305/10-1339/49. W. 192.5 cm. 61.40

*Madonna and Child.* Panel. School of Lippo Memmi, Italian, Siena, ca. 1317-1356. H. 71.3 cm. 52.110

*Two Female Saints.* Tempera and gold leaf on parchment. Niccolo di ser Sozzo Tegliacci, Italian, Siena, active 1334-1336. H. 8.3 cm. 24.430

*Madonna and Child with St. Catherine and St. John the Baptist.* Marble. Giovanni di Agostino, Italian, Siena, ca. 1310-1370. H. 69.8 cm. 42.1162

64

*Madonna and Child.* Marble. Ca. 1330s. Attr. to Andrea Pisano, Italian, Pisan-Florentine. H. 37.6 cm. 72.51

*Madonna and Child Enthroned.* Panel. Attr. to Master of the San Lucchese Altarpiece, Italian, Florence, mid-14th century. H. 113.7 cm. 68.206

*Leaf from an Antiphonary with The Coronation of the Virgin.* Tempera, ink, and gold leaf on parchment. Late 14th century. Attr. to Master of the Beffi Triptych (Abruzzi), Italian, Tuscany, H. 55.3 cm. 53.24

*Historiated Initial A from an Antiphonary.* Tempera, ink, and gold leaf on parchment. Signed and dated 1308. Neri da Rimini, Italian. H. 34.6 cm. 53.365

*Pair of Angels.* Marble. Ca. 1350. Attr. to Giovanni and Pacio da Firenze, Italian. H. 99.7 and 99.1 cm. 25.1343, 25.1344

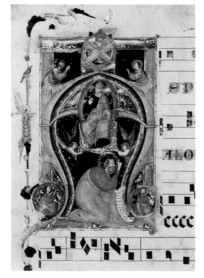

*Miniature from an Antiphonary:
Historiated Initial G with Christ
and Virgin in Glory.* Tempera and gold
leaf on parchment. Ca. 1390-1400.
Silvestro dei Gherarducci, Italian,
Florence. H. 34.9 cm. 30.105

*Partial Leaf from an Antiphonary
with Historiated Initial L with St.
Lucy.* Tempera, ink, and gold leaf on
parchment. Master of the Domincan
Effigies, Italian, ca. 1335-ca. 1345.
H. 44.3 cm. 52.281

*Crucifixion* (double-faced processional
cross). Panel. Anonymous Italian
Master, Venice, 14th century.
H. 61.3 cm. 43.280

*The Resurrection.* Embroidery, silk
on linen. Italy, Florence (Geri
Lapi?), 14th century. W. 42 cm.
29.904

*Navicella.* Pen and brown ink. Parri Spinelli, Italian,
ca. 1397-1453. W. 37.1 cm. 61.38

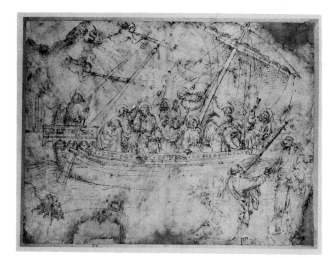

*Single Miniature from a Missal:*
*The Crucifixion.* Signed: Nicolaus F.
Tempera and gold leaf on parchment.
Niccolò da Bologna, Italian, active
ca. 1369-1402. H. 26 cm.  24.1013

*Crucifixion with the Two Thieves.*
Pen and brown ink and black chalk.
Altichiero Altichieri, Italian,
ca. 1330-1395. H. 24.4 cm.  56.43

*St. Francis before the Crucifix.*
Panel. Sassetta (Stefano di Giovanni),
Italian, Siena, 1392 (?)-1450.
H. 81 cm.  62.36

*Single Miniature Under Initial M:*
*The Annunciation.* Tempera and gold
leaf on parchment. North Italian,
ca. 1430-1440. H. 19.7 cm.  24.431

*Madonna and Child.* Pen and brown
ink on rose-tinted paper. Italy,
1440-1450. H. 10.7 cm.  56.42

*The Annunciation.* Lampas weave,
silk, linen, and gold. Italy, 2nd
half 14th century. Over-all:
W. 46.3 cm.  Detail: H. 22.9 cm.
31.61

*Adoration of the Magi.* Panel. Giovanni di Paolo,
Italian, Siena, ca. 1399-1482. W. 46.2 cm. 42.536

*Half of a Chasuble.* Cut velvet,
silk. Italy, early 15th century.
H. 108.5 cm. 43.66

*St. Catherine of Siena Invested with the
Dominican Habit.* Panel. Giovanni di Paolo,
Italian, Siena, ca. 1399-1482. H. 28.9 cm. 66.2

*St. Catherine of Siena and the Beggar.* Panel. Giovanni
di Paolo, Italian, Siena, ca. 1399-1482. W. 28.9 cm.
66.3

68

*Single Miniature of a Prophet from a Choral Book.* Tempera and gold leaf on parchment. Ca. 1420. Matteo Torelli, Italian, Florence. H. 16.7 cm. 49.536

*Madonna and Child Enthroned.* Panel. Master of 1419, Italian, Tuscany, active early 15th century. H. 196.2 cm. 54.834

*Hours of Charles the Noble: Page 165.* Miniature and Inhabited Acanthus Border by Master of Brussels Initials, Italian. Parchment, tempera, and gold. France, Paris, ca. 1405. H. 19.4 cm. 64.40

*The Madonna of Humility with the Temptation of Eve.* Panel. Carlo da Camerino, Italian, The Marches, active ca. 1380-1420. H. 191.2 cm. 16.795

*Girdle* (detail). Silver gilt and translucent enamel. Italy, Siena, late 14th century. L. approx. 236.8 cm. 30.742

*The Coronation of the Virgin.* Embroidery, silk, gold, and silver on linen. Italy, Florence, style of the School of Lorenzo Monaco, 1st half 15th century. D. 57.7 cm. 53.129

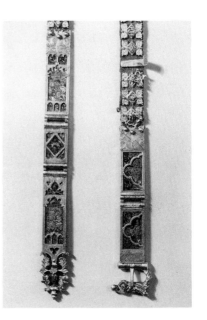

69

*Single Leaf from Gradual with Historiated Initial with Miniature of Virgin as Queen of Heaven.* Tempera and gold leaf on parchment. Italy, probably Milan, 2nd quarter 15th century. H. 56.2 cm. 28.652

*Cofanetto.* Painted and gilded wood. Italy, Siena. 14th century. H. 24.2 cm. 54.600

*Fragment of a Chasuble with Orphrey.* Lampas weave, silk and gold. Italy, 14th century. Orphrey: Compound twill, silk, linen, and gold. Germany, Cologne, late 14th century. Over-all: H. 106.8 cm. Detail: H. 44.5 cm. 28.653

*Textile.* Velvet weave, silk. Italy, Venice (?), 1st half 15th century. H. 38.5 cm. 18.310

*Single Leaf from a Treatise on Vices: Accidia and Her Court.* Brown ink, tempera, gold leaf on parchment. Italy, Genoa or Naples (?), late 14th century. H. 19 cm. 53.152

70

*Figured Medallion.* From a group of twelve medallions. Gold, enamel, and pearls. France, ca. 1400. D. 4.4 cm. 47.507

*Missal, For Paris Use (The Gotha Missal): fols. 63v-64r, The Crucifixion and Christ in Majesty.* Parchment; Latin written in two columns in red, blue, and brown, illuminated with tempera and gold leaf. Ca. 1360-1365. Jean Bondol, and his Atelier, French, Paris. H. 27.2 cm. 62.287

*Two Kneeling Carthusian Monks.* Marble. France, Paris, end of 14th century. H. 25.7 and 24.1 cm. 66.112, 66.113

*Mouton d'Or, Jean le Bon.* Gold. France, 1350-1364. D. 3 cm. 64.372

*The Calvary with a Carthusian Monk.*
Panel. Jean de Beaumetz. French,
Burgundy, active 1361/died 1396; and
Assistants. H. 56.5 cm. 64.454

*Hours of Charles the Noble: Page 395.*
Miniature by Egerton Master,
Netherlandish. Border by Master of
Brussels Initials, Italian. Parch-
ment, tempera, and gold. France,
Paris, ca. 1405. H. 19.4 cm. 64.360

*Table Fountain.* Silver gilt and
translucent enamel. France, late
14th century. H. 31.1 cm. 24.859

*Orphrey: Tree of Jesse.* Embroidery
*(opus Anglicanum),* silk, gold and
silver threads on linen. England,
mid-14th century. Over-all: H.
99 cm. Detail: H. 38 cm. 49.503

*Kneeling Figure.* From the Reliquary
of Saint Germain. Gilt bronze.
France, Paris, ca. 1408. H. 14 cm.
64.360

*The Annunciation.* Panel. Anonymous
French Master, Paris (?), Hainaut (?),
late 14th century. H. 35.2 cm.
54.393

*Triptych: Madonna and Child with Scenes of Annunciation, Visitation, Adoration, Presentation.* Ivory with gilding. France, late 14th century. H. 25.9 cm.  51.450

*Madonna and Child.* Painted limestone. France, Central Loire Valley, ca. 1385-1390. H. 54.6 cm. 62.28

*Three Mourners from the Tomb of Philip the Bold.* Vizelle alabaster (Grenoble stone). Early 15th century. Claus Sluter and Claus de Werve, Franco-Netherlandish. H. 41.6, 41.9, and 41.3 cm.  40.128, 58.66, 58.67

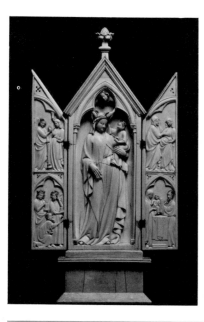

73

*The Coronation of the Virgin.* Panel.
The Rubielos Master, Spanish,
Valencia, active ca. 1400-1410.
H. 144.6 cm. 47.208

*A Bishop Saint with Donor.* Panel.
Anonymous Master, Spain (?), ca.
1420. H. 178 cm. 27.197

*Half of a Chasuble.* Velvet, cut
and voided, silk. Italy, 15th
century. Orphrey: embroidery,
silk and gold on linen. Austria,
Bohemia, 15th century. H. 119.3 cm.
50.85

*Madonna and Child from Mariapfarr
im Lungau.* Cast stone. Austria,
ca. 1395. H. 101.9 cm. 65.236

*Pietà (Vesperbild).* Painted cast stone. Austria,
Salzburg, ca. 1400-1425. H. 94 cm. 71.67

Triptych: *(House Altar).* Panel. Ca. 1425. Anonymous Austrian Master, Salzburg. W. 77.1 cm. 41.68

Diptych: *Four Scenes from the Passion.* Panel. Ca. 1400. Anonymous Austrian Master, Styria. W. 68.6 cm. 45.115

*Madonna and Child.* Painted lindenwood. Upper Austria, Diocese of Passau, ca. 1370-1380. H. 54 cm. 62.207

*The Coronation of the Virgin.* Panel. Master of the Fröndenberg Altarpiece, German, Westphalia, active early 15th century. H. 67.6 cm. 29.920

75

*The Death of the Virgin.* Panel.
Master of Heiligenkreuz, Austria,
ca. 1400. H. 71 cm. 36.496

Polyptych: *Passion of Christ.* Panel. Master of the Schlägl Altarpiece,
German, Westphalia, active ca. 1400-1450. W. 210.8 cm. 51.453

*Virgin Mary Crowned by Angels.* Panel.
Attr. to Stephen Lochner, German,
Cologne, died 1451. H. 50.5 cm.
68.20

*St. John the Baptist.* Panel. Robert
Campin, Netherlandish, Tournai,
ca. 1375-1444. W. 37.7 cm. 66.238

76

*Leaf from a Missal: Frontispiece for Canon of the Mass.* Tempera, gold leaf on parchment. N. Netherlands, Guelders-Overjissel, Cloister Agnietenberg near Zwolle, ca. 1438-1439. Miniature by Master of Otto von Moerdrecht. H. 33.3 cm. 59.254

*Lavabo.* Brass. South Netherlands, probably Valley of the Meuse, 15th century. H. 36.8 cm. 65.22

*The Adoration of the Magi.* Panel. Geertgen Tot Sint Jans, Netherlandish, Haarlem, ca. 1460-late 1480s. H. 29.2 cm. 51.353

*The Crucifixion.* Panel. Ca. 1470. Anonymous Master, Netherlands (?). H. 38.4 cm. 31.449

77

*Four Gospels.* Parchment, tempera, and gold leaf. Germany, Middle Rhine, ca. 1480. Miniatures by the Master of the Hausbuch. Contemporary blind-stamped leather binding. H. 22.9 cm. 52.465

*Madonna and Child with Saints.* Tapestry, wool, silk, and linen. Germany, Nuremberg, ca. 1490. W. 155.2 cm. 39.162

*The Adoration of the Magi.* Panel. Konrad Laib, Austrian, Vienna, active mid-15th century. H. 100 cm. 36.18

*Virgin Weeping.* Pearwood. Veit Stoss, German, 1447-ca. 1533. H. 31.4 cm. 39.64

*A Bridal Pair.* Panel. Anonymous South German Master, Upper Rhine Region, ca. 1470. H. 64.7 cm. 32.179

*The Nativity.* Panel. Ca. 1490.
Gerard David, Netherlandish, Bruges.
H. 85.2 cm.  58.320

*Hours of Ferdinand V and Isabella of Spain: fols. 72v and 73r, The Crucifixion and Deposition.* Parchment: Latin written in red and dark brown, illuminated with tempera and gold. Flanders, Ghent-Bruges School, ca. 1492-1504. H. 20 cm.  63.256

*The Annunciation.* Panel. Ca. 1480.
Aelbrecht Bouts, Netherlandish,
Louvain. H. 50.2 cm.  42.635

*Medallion: Annunciation.* Ivory.
Germany, Upper Rhine, ca. 1470.
D. 7 cm.  71.7

*Gothic Ornament of Oak-Leaf Design.*
Engraving. Master W with a Key.
Netherlandish, active ca. 1470.
H. 27.8 cm.  52.100

79

*St. John the Baptist.* Panel.
Dieric Bouts, Netherlandish, Louvain,
ca. 1415-1475. H. 106 cm. 51.354

*St. Andrew.* Oak with traces of paint.
North Netherlands, Region of Cleves,
early 16th century. H. 70.8 cm.
38.169

*Design for a Gothic Fountain.*
Engraving. Master W with a Key.
Netherlandish, active ca. 1470.
H. 23.3 cm. 37.565

*Monstrance with Relic of St.
Sebastian.* From the Guelph Treasure.
Silver gilt and crystal. Germany,
Brunswick, ca. 1475. H. 47 cm.
31.65

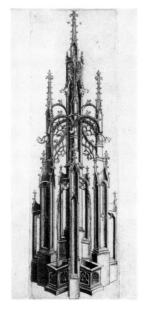

80

*Abbot's Stall.* Oak. France, 1500-1515. H. approx. 324.4 cm. 28.657

*Chest.* Painted wood. Spain, Catalan (?), late 15th century. H. 71.7 cm. 15.535

81

*Madonna and Child.* Panel. Follower
of Hans Memling, Netherlandish,
Bruges, ca. 1440-1494. H. 33.2 cm.
34.29

*The Mystical Grapes.* Tapestry, wool,
silk, and metallic threads. South
Netherlands, Flanders, ca. 1500.
H. 73.3 cm.  73.77

*Scenes from the Childhood of Christ.* Tapestry, wool, silk, and gold
metallic threads. South Netherlands, Flanders, late 15th century.
W. 2 m. 30.7 cm.  42.826

82

*Portrait of a Nobleman.* Panel.
Anonymous French Master, Burgundy (?),
ca. 1490-1500. H. 42.5 cm. 63.503

*The Story of Perseus and Andromeda.* Tapestry, wool
and silk. South Netherlands, Flanders, early 16th century.
W. 446.7 cm. 27.487

*Plate.* Inscribed: Maria. Majolica.
Spain, Valencia, Hispano-Moresque,
mid-15th century. D. 46.7 cm.
44.292

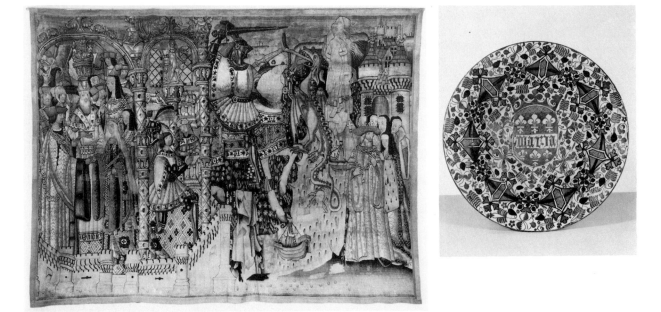

83

*The Annunciation to the Virgin.*
Panel. Jaime Ferrer II, Spanish,
Lérida, active mid-15th century.
H. 172.7 cm. 53.660

*A Monk at Prayer.* Panel. Anonymous
Master, Netherlandish, Bruges, early
16th century. H. 37.5 cm. 42.632

*Birth and Naming of Saint John the
Baptist.* Panel. Juan de Flandes,
Hispano-Flemish, ca. 1480-ca. 1519.
H. 88.4 cm. 75.3

*Portrait of a Lady.* Panel. Ca. 1480.
Anonymous Master, Netherlands (?).
H. 31.7 cm. 62.259

*Relief Heads of a Man and Woman.* Marble. France, Touraine, Circle of
Michel Colombe, 2nd decade 16th century. H. 14 cm. and 14.6 cm.
21.1003, 21.1004

84

*Holy Trinity.* Panel. Anonymous French Master, Provence (?), ca. 1470-1480. H. 119 cm. 60.79

*Triptych.* Onyx cameo. Italy, 13th century. Gold and translucent enamel. France, late 15th century. H. 5.7 cm. 47.508

*Mourner from the Tomb of Duke John the Fearless.* Vizelle alabaster (grenoble stone). Ca. 1462. Antoine le Moiturier, French. H. 41 cm. 40.129

*Education of the Virgin.* Limestone. France, Bourbonnais, early 16th century. H. 137.7 cm. 23.51

*Lady with Three Suitors.* Pen and brown ink and ink wash. France, ca. 1500. H. 23 cm. 56.40

85

*Miniature Showing Queen Medusa Enthroned.* Tempera on parchment. France, close to Maître François, ca. 1470. H. 12.7 cm. 24.1015

*Triumph of Eternity.* Tapestry, wool and silk, France, Valley of the Loire, 1500-1510. Over-all: W. 392.7 cm. Detail: W. 349.4 cm. 60.176

*Youth.* Tapestry, wool and silk. France, Valley of the Loire, 1500-1510. W. 462.5 cm. 60.177

*Time.* Tapestry, wool and silk. France, Valley of the Loire. 1500-1510. Over-all: W. 439.7 cm. Detail: W. 405.7 cm. 60.178

*St. John the Baptist Surrounded by the Evangelists and Four Fathers of the Latin Church.* Dated 1466. Engraving, state I/II. Master E. S., German. D. 18.3 cm.  50.585

*Playing Card with King and Helmet.* Engraving. Master E. S., German, active ca. 1450-1470. H. 9.6 cm.  49.564

*St. Jerome.* Dotted print colored by hand, state II/III. Germany, ca. 1470-1475. H. 35.6 cm.  52.13

*Christ Carrying His Cross.* Engraving. Martin Schongauer, German, before 1440-1491. W. 43.4 cm.  41.389

*An Angel Supporting Two Escutcheons.* Black chalk on pink-tinted paper. Germany, circle of Nicolaus Gerhaert von Leyden, ca. 1470. H. 21.2 cm.  62.205

87

*St. Jerome and the Lion.* Alabaster.
Ca. 1510. Tilmann Riemenschneider,
German. H. 37.8 cm. 46.82

*Corpus of Christ.* Lindenwood.
Ca. 1525-1530. Hans Leinberger,
Germany, Bavaria, Landshut.
H. 118.1 cm. 38.293

*The Organ Player and His Wife.*
Engraving, state I/III. Israhel
van Meckenem, German, before 1450-
1503. H. 16.7 cm. 60.73

*The Flight into Egypt.* Engraving.
Martin Schongauer, German, before
1440-1491. H. 25.5 cm. 54.260

*St. Lawrence* and *St. Stephen.* Lindenwood. 1502-1510. Tilmann
Riemenschneider, German. H. 94.6 and 92.7 cm. 59.42, 59.43

88

*The Mass of St. Gregory.* Panel. Hans Baldung (called Grien), German, 1484/85-1545. W. 124.9 cm. 52.112

*The Bewitched Groom.* Woodcut. 1544. Hans Baldung (called Grien), German. H. 33.8 cm. 66.172

*Pietà (Vesperbild).* Painted and gilded lindenwood. Ca. 1515-1520. Master of Rabenden, German, Bavaria, Chiemgau. H. 89.1 cm. 38.294

*John VIII Palaeologus.* Emperor of Constantinople, 1425-1428. Lead medal. Antonio di Puccio Pisano (called Pisanello), Italian, Pisa, ca. 1395-Rome 1455. D. 10.4 cm. 74.109

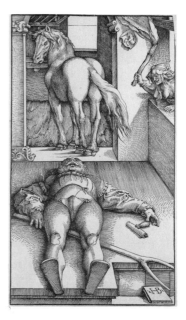

89

*Oak-Leaf Jar.* Majolica. Italy, Florence, or Montelupo, 2nd quarter 15th century. H. 20.4 cm. 43.54

*Portrait of a Man.* Panel. Colantonio (?), Italian, Naples, active ca. 1430/40-ca. 1460/70. H. 60 cm. 16.811

*Fragmentary Head of a Cherub.* Marble. Italy, Florence, 3rd quarter 15th century. H. 18.4 cm. 68.211

*Leonella d'Este, Marquess of Ferrara.* Bronze. Ca. 1440-1444. Antonio di Puccio Pisano (called Pisanello), Italian. D. 6.9 cm. 71.4

*Double Mazer.* Maple with silver-gilt mounts. Germany, ca. 1530. With portrait medallion (1528) of Albrecht Dürer by Matthes Gebel, Nuremberg and Augsburg. H. 24.8 cm. 50.83

90

*The Funeral of St. Stephen.* Pen and bistre ink. Fra Filippo Lippi, Italian, 1406-1469. H. 25.1 cm. 47.70

*St. Anthony Abbot.* Panel. 1457-1458. Fra Filippo Lippi, Italian, Florence. H. 81.3 cm. 64.151

*Head of a Man, an Angel, and Two Small Profile Heads.* Silverpoint heightened with white, on rose prepared paper. Italy, circle of Benozzo Gozzoli, 1420-1497. H. 19.4 cm. 37.24

*St. Michael.* Panel. 1457-1458. Fra Filippo Lippi, Italian, Florence. H. 81.3 cm. 64.150

*Head of a Boy.* Marble. Italy, Florence, ca. 1470. H. 24.3 cm. 31.454

*Madonna and Child with Angels.* Panel. Italy, Florence, after Fra Filippo Lippi, ca. 1406-1469. H. 94.9 cm. 16.802

91

*Front Cover for a Gospel Book of Cardinal Jean Balue.* Silver and niello with silver-gilt border. Italy, Florence, ca. 1467-1469. H. 41.6 cm. 52.109

*Battle of Naked Men.* Engraving, state I. Antonio Pollaiuolo, Italian, 1431/32-1498. W. 60.7 cm. 67.127

*Madonna and Child.* Panel. Francesco Botticini, Italian, Florence, ca. 1446-1497. H. 96.7 cm. 16.789

*Textile.* Velvet weave, silk. Italy, early 15th century. H. 44.5 cm. 40.370

*Pax: Madonna and Child.* Gilt bronze, silver and blue enamel. Last quarter 15th century. After Antonio Rossellino, Italian, Florence. H. 15.9 cm. 68.24

*Madonna and Child.* Painted terra cotta. Ca. 1475. Antonio Rossellino and his workshop, Italian, Florence. H. 91.4 cm. 42.780

*Madonna and Child.* Silverpoint on rose prepared paper. Lorenzo di Credi, Italian, 1459/60-1537. H. 14.5 cm. 63.472

*St. Jerome in Penitence.* Engraving. Italy, Florence, ca. 1480-1500. W. 21.5 cm. 49.33

*Madonna and Child with the Young St. John.* Tondo. Panel. Sandro Botticelli, Italian, Florence, 1444-1510. D. 68 cm. 70.160

93

*Page from a Prayer Book.* Tempera and gold leaf on parchment. Attavante degli Attavanti, Italian, Florence, 1452-1520/25. H. 15.2 cm. 53.280

*The Assumption of the Virgin.* Engraving, state I/II, ca. 1490. Attributed to Francesco Rosselli, Italian. H. 81.6 cm. 49.32

*Life of the Virgin and of Christ: The Agony in the Garden.* Engraving, state I/III. Attributed to Francesco Rosselli, Italian, 1448-before 1513. H. 22.4 cm. 49.540

*The Last Supper.* Engraving. Lucantonio degli Uberti, Italian, active ca. 1495-1520. W. 106.6 cm. 40.473-a

*The Holy Family with the Infant St. John and St. Margaret.* Tondo. Panel. Filippino Lippi, Italian, Florence, ca. 1457-1504. D. 153 cm. 32.227

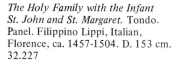

*Standing Figure of a Man.* Bronze. Ca. 1500. Circle of Francesco di Giorgio, Italian, Siena. H. 31 cm. 47.509

*Bust of Christ.* Painted terra cotta. Italy, Florence, late 15th century. H. 55.9 cm. 21.956

*Christ Child.* Marble. Ca. 1490-1500. Attr. to Michele (Di Luca) Marini, Italian. H. 87.6 cm. 75.47

*St. John.* Terra cotta. Master of the Statuettes of St. John, Italian, Florence, active ca. 1500. H. 72.1 cm. 42.781

*Paneling from a Sacristy Bench* (detail). Walnut, inlaid with holly and ebony. Italy, Florence, late 15th century. L. 173.3 cm. 15.526

*St. Sebastian.* Brush and brown ink over silverpoint on prepared paper. Pietro Perugino, Italian, 1445/50-1523. H. 25.6 cm. 58.411

*Madonna and Child with St. Anthony Abbot, St. Sebastian, St. Mark, and St. Severino.* Panel. Lorenzo d'Alessandro da Sanseverino, Italian, Umbria. Active 1468-1503. H. 128.9 cm. 16.800

*The Crucifixion.* Panel. Matteo di Giovanni di Bartolo, Italian, Siena, ca. 1430-1495. W. 31 cm. 40.535

*Single Leaf from an Antiphonary: Adoration of the Shepherds.* Tempera and gold leaf on parchment. Ca. 1470. Italy, Siena, style nearest to Guidoccio Cozzarelli or Matteo Giovanni. H. 57.2 cm. 52.282

*Single Miniature: Christ on the Mount of Olives.* Tempera on parchment. Ca. 1490-1500. Attr. to Timoteo Viti, Italian, Umbia. H. 27 cm. 27.161

*The Lamentation.* Tapestry, wool, silk, gold, and silver. Italy, Ferrara, after design by Cosimo Tura, ca. 1475. W. 197 cm. 50.145

*Leaf from a Gradual: Historiated Initial M.* Tempera and gold leaf on parchment. Attr. to Cosimo Tura, Italian, Ferrara, 1432-1495. H. 76.8 cm. 27.425

*Antiphonary.* Tempera and gold leaf on parchment. Antonio Liberale da Verona, Italian, 1445-ca. 1526. Detail: H. 18.4 cm. 30.661

*Jar with Portrait.* Majolica. Italy, Caffaggiolo, ca. 1475-1480. H. 30.5 cm. 41.550

*Adoration of the Christ Child.*
Marble with some gilding. Italy,
Lombardy, late 15th century.
Workshop of Benedetto Briosco and
Tommaso Cazzaniga. H. 61 cm.
28.863

*Holy Family with a Shepherd.* Canvas.
Dosso Dossi (Giovanni di Lutero),
Italian, active 1512, died 1542.
H. 38.7 cm. 49.185

*Plate.* Majolica. Italy, Faenza,
late 15th century. D. 35.6 cm.
23.915

*Drug Bottle.* Majolica. Italy,
Faenza, ca. 1480. H. 38.7 cm.
43.52

*Dancing Boy.* Bronze. North Italy,
ca. 1500. H. 10.3 cm. 75.29

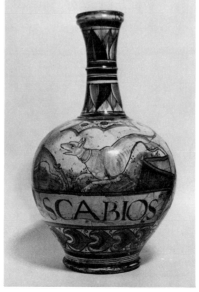

*Single Miniature: The Nativity.*
Tempera and gold on parchment.
Girolamo dai Libri, Italian, Verona,
1474-1555. H. 16.4 cm. 53.281

*Mother and Child with Two Dogs.*
Engraving. Italy, late 15th century.
W. 14.9 cm. 37.566

*Madonna and Child.* Marble. Circle
of Bartolommeo Bellano, Italian,
Padua, ca. 1435-1496/97. H. 54.6 cm.
20.273

*The Adoration of the Magi, the
Virgin in the Grotto.* Engraving.
Italy, Mantegna School, after 1463.
H. 39.4 cm. 54.66

*Pietà.* Tempera on parchment.
Attributed to Andrea Mantegna,
Italian, 1431-1506. H. 14.1 cm.
51.394

99

*St. Christopher.* Pen and brown ink with blue and green washes, touches of white. Andrea Mantegna, Italian, 1431-1506. H. 28.7 cm. 56.39

*Hercules and Antaeus.* Engraving. Italy, Mantegna School, 15th century. H. 25.3 cm. 64.32

*A Fallen Warrior.* Blackened wax. Ca. 1500. Close to Leonardo da Vinci, Italian. H. 19.1 cm. 63.576

*Farm on the Slope of a Hill.* Pen and brown ink. Fra Bartolommeo, Italian, 1472-1517. W. 29.4 cm. 57.498

100

*Adoration of the Magi.* Bronze. Ca. 1500-1506. Andrea
Briosco (called Riccio), Italian, Padua. H. 23.5 cm.
54.601

*Tarocchi Cards (E Series): Music.*
Engraving, touched with gold. Italy,
Ferrara, not later than 1467.
H. 18.1 cm.  24.457

*Base for a Satyr and Satyress
Group.* Bronze. Andrea Briosco
(called Riccio), Italian, Padua,
ca. 1470/75-1532. H. 32.7 cm.
50.375

*Pomona.* Bronze. Ca. 1500. Andrea
Briosco (called Riccio), Italian,
Padua. H. 15.5 cm.  48.486

101

*Battle in a Wood.* Engraving. Master of the Year 1515,
Italian. W. 31.5 cm. 49.34

*Satyress Triumphant.* Bronze.
Ca. 1520-1530. Andrea Briosco
(called Riccio), Italian, Padua.
H. 16.5 cm. 47.29

*Marriage Beaker.* Enameled milk
glass. Italy, Venice, late 15th
century. H. 10.2 cm. 55.70

*Portrait of a Nun of the Order of
San Secondo.* Panel. Jacometto
Veneziano, Italian, Venice, active
1472-died before 1498. H. 24.1 cm.
76.9

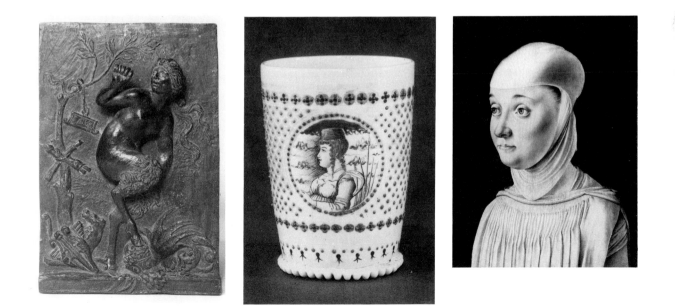

102

*Sacred Conversation: The Virgin and Child with St. Anthony Abbot and
St. Lucy (?) with Donors.* Panel. Giovanni Battista Cima da Conegliano,
Italian, Venice, 1459-1517 or 1518. W. 80 cm. 42.636

*Portrait of a Youth.* Panel.
Bartolommeo Veneto, Italia, Venice,
1st half 16th century.
H. 41.9 cm. 40.539

*St. Nicholas of Bari.* Panel.
Carlo Giovanni Crivelli, Italian,
Venice, ca. 1430/35-ca. 1495.
H. 97.3 cm. 52.111

*Plate.* Majolica. Italy, Deruta,
early 16th century. D. 41.3 cm.
23.1096

103

*Tabernacle Relief* (detail).
Polychromed marble. North Italian,
late 15th century. H. 81.3 cm.
75.105

*Bird's-Eye View of Venice* (detail). Dated 1500. Woodcut, state I/III.
Jacopo de' Barbari, Italian. W. 100.3 cm. 49.569

*Pedlar Goblet.* Enameled green and
blue glass. Italy, Venice, ca. 1475.
H. 18.9 cm. 53.364

*Albarello.* Majolica. Italy, Faenza,
early 16th century. H. 29.8 cm.
40.12

*Plate: The Prodigal Son, after Dürer.*
Majolica. Signed and dated 1528.
Maestro Giorgio, Italian, Faenza (?).
D. 21.2 cm. 50.82

104

*Tazza with Putti Frieze.* Enameled
blue glass. Italy, Venice, ca.
1490. H. 18.3 cm. 60.38

*Ewer.* Painted enamel on copper.
Italy, Venice, ca. 1500. H. 18.8 cm.
23.720

*Textile Panel.* Cut velvet weave,
silk and gold. Italy, 15th
century. Over-all: H. 301 cm.
Detail: H. 150 cm. 73.20

*Philoctetes on the Island of Lemnos.*
Marble. Antonio Lombardo, Italian,
Paduan-Venetian, ca. 1458-ca. 1516 (?)
H. 23.3 cm. 73.168

*Man with an Arrow.* Engraving,
state II/II. Benedetto Montagna,
Italian, ca. 1470-after 1540.
H. 21 cm. 43.65

105

*Textile.* Velvet weave, cut and brocaded, silk and gold. Italy, 15th century. H. 150 cm.  31.63

*Running Woman.* Bronze. Italy, Padua, ca. 1527. H. 18.2 cm.  63.92

*Plate: The Three Graces.* Majolica. 1525. Maestro Giorgio (Giorgio Andreoli da Gubbio), Italian, Gubbio. D. 44.8 cm.  45.2

*Venus Prudentia.* Gilt bronze. Attr. to Tullio Lombardo, Italian, Venice, ca. 1455-1532. H. 18.3 cm.  48.171

*Venus Reclining in a Landscape.* Engraving, state I/II. Giulio Campagnola, Italian, ca. 1482-after 1515. W. 18.4 cm.  31.205

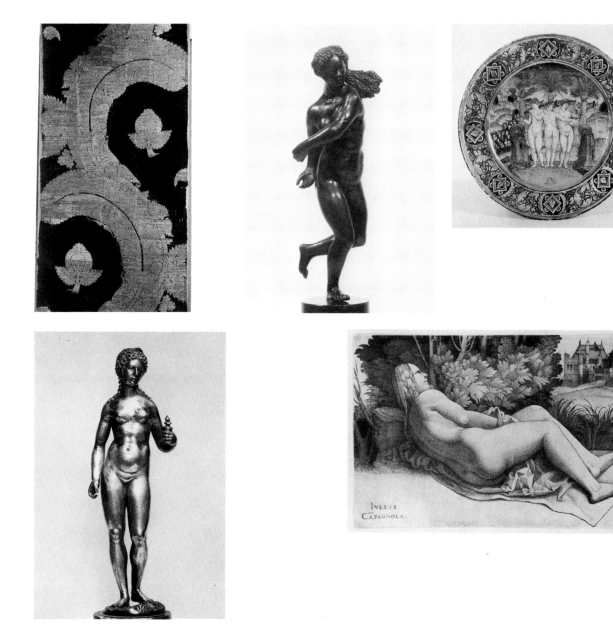

*Madonna and Child.* From Ciborium of Cardinal d'Estouteville in S. Maria Maggiore, Rome. Marble. Ca. 1461-1464. Mino del Reame (?), Italian. H. 93.7 cm. 28.747

*Study for the Nude Youth over the Prophet Daniel, in the Sistine Chapel Ceiling Fresco.* Red chalk. Michelangelo Buonarroti, Italian, 1475-1564. H. 33.5 cm. 40.465

*Figure of Plenty (Dovizia).* Glazed terra cotta. Late 1520s. Giovanni della Robbia, Italian. H. 110.2 cm. 40.343

*Portrait of a Nobleman.* Canvas. Lorenzo Lotto, Italian, Venice, 1480-1556. H. 109 cm. 50.250.

107

*The Sacrifice of Isaac.* Panel.
Andrea del Sarto, Italian, Florence,
1486-1530. H. 178.2 cm. 37.577

*Madonna and Child.* Bronze. Ca. 1527.
Signed Jacopo Tatti (called Sansovino),
Italian. H. 47.6 cm. 51.316

*The Fate of the Evil Tongue.*
Engraving. Nicoletto Rosex
da Modena, Italian, active ca.
1490-after 1511. H. 29.3 cm. 47.11

*Majolica Plate.* Dated 1526. Signed:
M. G. da Agubio. Maestro Giorgio,
Italian. D. 27 cm. 50.156

108

*Circular Table.* Walnut. Italy, Florence, 3rd quarter
16th century. H. 80 cm. 39.183

*Majolica Albarello: Andromeda Saved by Perseus.* Italy, Venice, Workshop of Domenigo da Venezia, early 16th century. H. 28.9 cm. 20.421

*Venus.* Bronze. Ca. 1560. Danese Cattaneo, Italian. H. 52.9 cm. 50.578

*St. John the Baptist.* Bronze. Angelo de Rossi, Italian, Verona, active late 16th century. H. 49.5 cm. 52.276

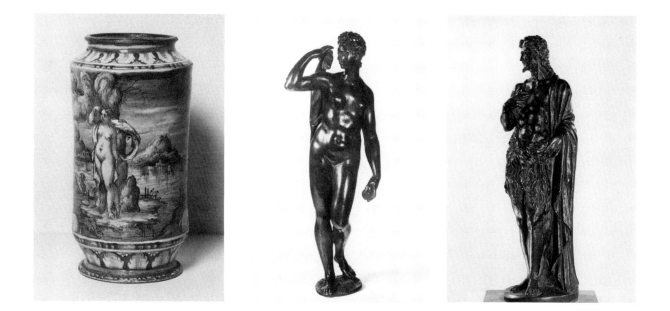

109

*Adoration of the Magi.* Canvas. Titian (Tiziano Vecelli), Italian, Venice, ca. 1488-1576. W. 228.3 cm. 57.150

*Doorknocker with Gorgon Head and Emblem of the Cicogna Family.* Bronze. Italy, Venice, mid-16th century. H. 25.4 cm. 72.1

*Baptism of Christ.* Canvas. After 1580. Tintoretto (Jacopo Robusti), Italian, Venice. W. 251.4 cm. 50.400

110

*Virgin and Child Enthroned.* Verre
eglomisé. Italy, 2nd half 16th
century. Frame: Silver and enamel.
Germany, Augsburg, ca. 1600.
H. 18.8 cm. 43.284

*St. Margaret.* Marble. 1520-1530.
Antonello Gagini, Italian, Sicilian.
H. 139.7 cm. 42.564

*Pendant: Madonna and Child with
Saints.* Enameled gold with pearls
and emeralds. Italy, late 16th
century. H. 7.3 cm. 59.337

*The Assumption of the Virgin.*
Dated 1517. Engraving, state
I/II. Domenico Campagnola,
Italian. H. 29.2 cm. 54.741

111

*The Dead Christ with Joseph of Arimathea.* Panel. Ca. 1525. Giovanni
Girolamo Savoldo, Italian, Brescia. W. 191.8 cm. 52.512

*Head of St. John the Baptist.*
Canvas. Ca. 1580. Circle of
Titian, Italian, Venice.
W. 75.2 cm. 53.424

*Credenza.* Walnut. Italy, Brescia, mid-16th century.
H. 127.6 cm. 39.188

*Majolica Plate.* Italy, Urbino
Atelier of the Fontana Family,
ca. 1560. D. 45.7 cm. 42.622

*Portrait of Agostino Barbarigo.* Canvas. Ca. 1571.
Paolo Veronese, Italian, Venice. W. 116.2 cm.
28.16

*Apollo on Parnassus, Surrounded by Muses and Poets.*
Engraving, before state I/II. Marcantonio Raimondi,
Italian, ca. 1480-ca. 1530. W. 47.1 cm. 63.231

*Portrait of a Young Lady.* Panel.
Agnolo Bronzino, Italian, Florence,
1503-1572. H. 60 cm. 72.121

*Portrait of Vincenzo Guarignoni.*
Dated 1572. Canvas. Giovanni
Battista Moroni, Italian, Bergamo.
H. 63 cm. 62.1

*Cassone Frontal.* Walnut. Italy, second half 16th century. L. 172.7 cm.
15.528

*Portrait of a Gentleman and His Wife.* Canvas.
Ca. 1550-1565. Italo-Flemish Master. W. 141 cm.
16.793

114

*Lazarus and the Rich Man.* Canvas. Jacopo Bassano, Italian. 1510-1592.
W. 221 cm. 39.68

*The Wrath of Neptune.* Bronze.
Ca. 1540. Attr. to Tiziano Minio,
Italian, Paduan-Venetian.
H. 36.1 cm. 74.273

*The Entombment.* Canvas. Leandro
Bassano, Italian, 1557-1622.
H. 123.8 cm. 16.806

*Annunciation.* Canvas. Paolo
Veronese, Italian, Venice, 1528-
1588. H. 150 cm. 50.251

*Annunciation.* Pen and brown ink
and gray wash. Luca Cambiaso,
Italian, 1527-1585. H. 29.5 cm.
59.200

115

*Landscape with a Boat.* Pen and brown ink. Annibale
Carracci, Italian, 1560-1609. W. 40.6 cm. 72.101

*Cassone.* Walnut. Italy, Venice, mid-16th century.
H. 68.6 cm. 42.607

*The Feast of the Gods.* Bronze.
Ca. 1575. Alessandro Vittoria,
Italian, Venetian. H. 34.4 cm.
52.464

116

*Medici Plate.* Soft paste porcelain.
Italy, Florence, ca. 1580.
D. 28 cm. 49.489

*Study for Aeneas' Flight from Troy.* Pen and brown ink,
black chalk, brown and light-yellow wash on gray-green
paper. Federico Barocci, Italian, 1535 (?)-1612.
W. 42.7 cm. 60.26

*Mars.* Bronze. Ca. 1587. Giovanni
Bologna, Italian. H. 39 cm. 64.421

*Study of Plants on a Bank.* Black
chalk, brush and wash heightened
with body color. Federico Barocci,
Italian, ca. 1535-1612. H. 20 cm.
73.171

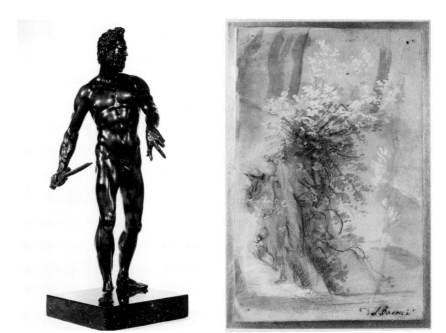

117

*Hat Jewel: The Rape of Helen.*
Enamel on gold. Italy, mid-16th
century. D. 5.1 cm. 49.377

*Hat Jewel: Adoration of the Kings.*
Enamel on gold. France, mid-16th
century. D. 4.7 cm. 38.428

*Espalier Plates.* Steel. Attributed
to a member of Negroli Family,
possibly Philippo, ca. 1500-1561,
Italian, Milan. H. 14 cm.
16.1517, 16.1518

*The Apocalypse: St. John Sees the
Four Riders.* Engraving. Jean Duvet,
French, 1485-after 1556. H. of
page 36.7 cm. 53.222

*Episode of the Aeneid: The Trojan
Horse.* Painted enamel. Ca. 1530-
1540. Master of the Aeneid Series,
France, Limoges. H. 23.8 cm.
74.40

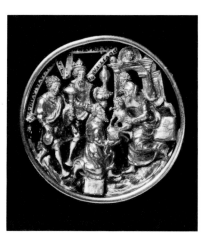

118

*Chest.* Oak. France, Normandy, 2nd half 16th century. H. 96.5 cm. 42.604

*Two Funerary Figures.* Hawthorn wood painted black. Ca. 1570. Attr. to Germain Pilon, French. H. 62.2 and 61.3 cm. 59.345, 59.346

*Seated Woman with Two Children (Charity?).* Alabaster. Attr. to Germain Pilon, French, ca. 1535-1590. H. 29.8 cm. 51.541

*St. Porchaire Pedestal Dish.* Faience. France, 16th century. H. 14.3 cm. 52.278

*St. Porchaire Ewer.* Faience. France, 16th century. H. 35.6 cm. 53.363

*Mirror.* Enamel "en risille." France, 2nd half 16th century. H. 8.9 cm. 26.246

*Ewer Stand.* Enamel on copper. Dated 1577. Pierre Raymond, French, Limoges. D. 48.6 cm. 40.139

*Inlaid Table.* Walnut. France, Burgundy, 2nd half 16th century. H. 88.3 cm. 42.601

*Dressoir.* Walnut. France, Burgundy, mid-16th century. H. 149.8 cm. 42.606

*The Martyrdom of St. Lucy.* Etching,
state II/II. Jacques Bellange,
French, 1594-1638. H. 46.2 cm.
50.214

*Samson and Delilah.* Woodcut.
Lucas van Leyden, Dutch, 1494-1533.
H. 41.3 cm. 35.117

*Candlesticks Representing Triumph of
Diana and Labors of Hercules.* Painted
enamel on copper. Attr. to Jean Court
(called Vigier), French, Limoges, active
1555-1565. H. 33.6 cm. 73.169, 73.170

*Adoration of the Shepherds.*
Engraving. Frans Crabbe, Flemish,
ca. 1480-1553. H. 24.6 cm. 66.121

*Return of the Prodigal Son.* Engraving. Lucas van
Leyden, Dutch, 1494-1533. W. 24.6 cm. 27.361

*Landscape with Saint John the Baptist Preaching.* Panel.
Herri met de Bles, Netherlandish, ca. 1510-ca. 1572.
W. 42 cm. 67.20

*Madonna and Child under a Canopy.*
Panel. Ca. 1525. Netherlands,
Bruges. H. 64.8 cm. 46.282

*Esther before Ahasuerus* and *The Judgment of Solomon.* Stained glass panels.
Ca. 1530. Circle of Lucas van Leyden, Netherlandish. H. 69.2 cm.
68.189, 68.188

122

*Christ Carrying the Cross.* Alabaster.
Ca. 1545. Workshop of Jacques du
Broeucq, Southern Netherlands,
Hainaut. H. 61.1 cm. 71.5

*Madonna and Child in a Landscape.*
Dated 1531. Panel. Jan Gossaert
de Mabuse, Netherlandish.
H. 48.9 cm. 72.47

*Landscape with Venus and Adonis.* Copper panel. Gillis
van Coninxloo, Netherlandish, 1544-1606/07. W. 53.5 cm.
62.293

*Two Peasants in Half Figure.*
Pen and light brown ink over black
chalk. Pieter Bruegel I, Flemish,
1525-1569. W. 18.8 cm. 45.114

*Diana and Actaeon.* Canvas. Joachim Uytewael, Dutch. 1566-1638. W. 69 cm. 74.106

*Denial of St. Peter.* Panel. Peter Uytewael, Dutch, 1596-1660. W. 45.6 cm. 72.169

*Part of a Chasuble.* Embroidery *(opus Anglicanum),* silk, gold, and silver threads on silk velvet. England, ca. 1500. H. 101 cm. 70.124

*Portrait of an Elizabethan Gallant.* Dated 1576. On vellum. Nicholas Hilliard, English. D. 5 cm. 60.39

*Sir Anthony Mildmay.* On vellum. Nicholas Hilliard, English, Ca. 1547-1619. H. 23.5 cm. 26.554

124

*The Ascension.* Pen and brown ink.
Albrecht Dürer, German, 1471-1528.
H. 31.1 cm. 52.530

*The Apocalypse: The Riders on the
Four Horses.* Woodcut. Albrecht
Dürer, German, 1471-1528.
H. 40 cm. 32.313

*The Virgin with a Monkey.* Engraving.
Albrecht Dürer, German, 1471-1528.
H. 19.1 cm. 64.29

*The Arm of Eve.* Dated 1507.
Brush drawing in brown and white ink
on blue paper. Albrecht Dürer,
German. H. 33.6 cm. 65.470

*The Dead Christ.* Dated 1505. Charcoal. Albrecht
Dürer, German. W. 23.5 cm. 52.531

125

*St. Jerome.* Engraving. Albrecht Dürer, German, 1471-1528. H. 24.5 cm. 72.29

*Adoration of the Shepherds.* Panel. Circle of Dürer, Germany, 1st half 16th century. H. 58 cm. 16.807

*Plaque: Christ in the Garden of Gethsemane.* Kelheim stone. Ca. 1515. Adolph Daucher, German, Augsburg, d. ca. 1523. H. 14.8 cm. 47.182

*Christ on the Mount of Olives.* Dated 1515. Etching on iron. Albrecht Dürer, German. H. 22.3 cm. 43.389

*The Life of the Virgin: Title Page, The Virgin on the Crescent Moon.* Woodcut, proof before text. Albrecht Dürer, German, 1471-1528. H. 24 cm. 59.99

126

*Adam and Eve.* Bronze. Dated 1515 (for the model); on reverse 1518 (for this cast). Ludwig Krug, German, Nuremberg. H. 12.2 cm.

*Pyramus and Thisbe.* Chiaroscuro woodcut. Hans Wechtlin, German, 1480/85-after 1526. H. 27.1 cm. 50.396

*Der Weisskunig: The Banished Duke of Otnop.* Woodcut. Hans Burgkmair, German, 1473-1531. H. 22.2 cm. 60.28

*Adam and Eve.* Bronze. Ca. 1520. Workshop of Peter Vischer, the Younger, German, Nuremberg. H. 14.6 cm. 61.29

*Adam and Eve.* Boxwood. Attributed to Daniel Mauch, German, 1477-1540. H. 22.2 cm. 46.429, 46.491

*Portrait of Wolfgang Gamensfelder at Age 19.* Boxwood. Dated 1531. Master of Gamensfelder and Fronleitner, German. D. 11.9 cm. 76.16

*Head of a Woman.* Silverpoint on white prepared ground on paper. Hans Holbein I, German, ca. 1465-1524. H. 6.5 cm. 70.14

*Portrait of Sir Thomas More.* Panel. Follower of Hans Holbein the Younger, Germany, 1497-1543. D. 5.9 cm. 57.356

*Equestrian Portrait of the Emperor Maximilian.* Dated 1508. Woodcut printed from two outline blocks on blue hand-tinted paper. Hans Burgkmair, German. H. 32.1 cm. 50.72

*Armet, Helmet in Maximilian Style.* Steel. Germany, early 16th century. H. 30.5 cm. 16.1855

*Portrait Medallion.* Boxwood. Attr. to Friedrich Hagenauer, German, active 1525-1546. D. 7.3 cm. 27.421

*The Stag Hunt.* Dated 1540. Panel. Lucas Cranach the Elder, German, Kronach. W. 170.2 cm. 58.425

*Medal: The Trinity.* Silver. Signed H. R. Dated 1544. Hans Reinhart the Elder, German, d. 1581. D. 10.2 cm. 60.74

129

*Fountain Figure of Abundance.*
Bronze. Master of the Budapest
Abundance, German, Augsburg, ca.
1530-1540. H. 36.8 cm. 71.104

*Horse.* Bronze. Ca. 1560-1570. After Gregor Erhart,
German. H. 15.2 cm. 52.108

*Sitting Dog Scratching Himself.*
Bronze. South Germany or possibly
Austria (Innsbruck), 2nd quarter
16th century. H. 5.9 cm. 60.74

130

*Portrait Plaque of Georg Knauer.*
Pearwood. Dated 1537. Peter Dell,
South German. H. 14 cm. 27.427

*Portrait of Maria Kitscher von
Oelkofen, Frau Pancraz von Freyberg
zu Aschau.* Panel. Hans Mielich,
German, Munich, 1515-1573.
H. 64.1 cm. 44.88

*Model for Medal: Pope Alexander V
(1409-1410).* Kelheim stone. Tobias
Wolf, German, Breslau, d. ca. 1570.
D. 4.2 cm. 56.28

*Model for Medal: Son of Martin III
Geuder.* Kelheim stone. Dated 1528.
Matthes Gebel, German, Nuremberg.
D. 3.7 cm. 56.25

131

*Salome with the Head of St. John the Baptist.* Pen and brush with black and white ink on brown-tinted paper. Albrecht Altdorfer, German, ca. 1480-1538. H. 19.2 cm. 48.440

*The Fall and Redemption of Man: Four Scenes from the Passion of Christ.* Four woodcuts printed on one page. Albrecht Altdorfer, German, ca. 1480-1538. H. of page 22.5 cm. 52.50-52.53

*The Visitation.* Panel. Germany, Danube School, early 16th century. H. 101.6 cm. 50.91

*View of a Castle.* Dated 1513. Pen and bistre ink. Wolf Huber, German, Passau. W. 21.2 cm. 51.277

*Mortar.* Bronze. Ca. 1550-1560. Workshop of Wenzel Jamnitzer, German, Nuremberg, H. 11.8 cm. 51.444

*River Landscape with Five Bare Spruce Trees in the Foreground.* Dated 1549. Etching. Augustin Hirschvogel, German. W. 17.3 cm.  51.491

*Jug with Arms of Cleves-Berg.* Stoneware. Dated 1580. Germany, Rhenish, Siegberg. H. 23.8 cm. 74.41

133

*Standing Cup with Cover.* Gilt silver. Germany, Nuremberg, 2nd half 16th century. H. 49.5 cm. 62.286

*Scales.* Gilt bronze and engraved silver. Ca. 1565-1570. Germany, Nuremberg, Jamnitzer Workshop. H. 37.5 cm. 50.382

*Double Pokal.* Gilt silver. Ca. 1614-1632. Alexander Treghart, South German, Nuremberg. H. 58 cm. 76.108, 76.109

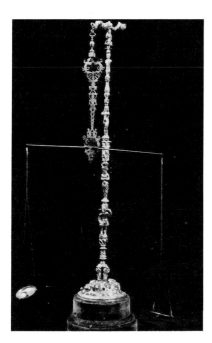

*Sextus Tarquinius Threatening Lucrece.* Bronze. Ca. 1600. Hubert Gerhard, German. H. 52.7 cm. 62.245

*Pendant with Pelican.* Enameled gold with rubies. Germany, ca. 1600. H. 7.3 cm. 59.336

*Hercules and the Hydra.* Bronze. Attr. to Adriaen de Vries, Netherlandish, ca. 1560-1626. H. 46.7 cm. 73.167

*Allegory of Christian Belief.* Dated 162(2?). Pen and bistre ink and bistre wash. Johann Liss, German. H. 15.3 cm. 53.6

*Amor.* Canvas. Johann Liss, German, Venetian School, ca. 1597-1629/30. H. 87.6 cm. 71.100

135

*The Crucifixion of St. Andrew.* Canvas. Ca. 1607. Michelangelo Merisi da Caravaggio, Italian. H. 202.5 cm. 76.2

*Head of Proserpine.* Terra cotta. Ca. 1620-1621. Giovanni Lorenzo Bernini, Italian, Rome. H. 15.3 cm. 68.101

*Danaë.* Canvas. Ca. 1621-1623. Orazio Gentileschi, Italian. W. 228.6 cm. 71.101

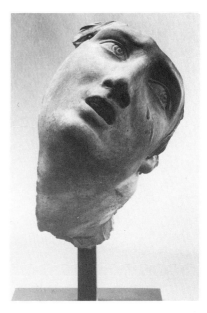

136

*Study for Minerva.* Black and red chalk. Bernardo Strozzi, Italian, 1581-1644. H. 37.2 cm. 53.626

*Minerva.* Canvas. Bernardo Strozzi, Italian, Genoa, 1581-1644. H. 147.3 cm. 29.133

*Venus and Cupid.* Pen and bistre ink and bistre wash with red chalk indications. Giovanni Francesco Barbieri (called Guercino), Italian, 1591-1666. W. 39.4 cm. 25.1188

*Rest on the Flight into Egypt with an Angel Playing the Violin.* Tondo. Canvas. 1624. Giovanni Francesco Barbieri (called Il Guercino), Italian. D. 68.5 cm. 67.123

137

*Adoration of the Shepherds.* Canvas. Bernardo Cavallino,
Italian, 1616-1656. W. 148.6 cm. 68.100

*Pope Innocent X.* Bronze.
Alessandro Algardi and assistants,
Italian, Rome, 1602-1654.
H. 78.1 cm. 57.496

*Adoration of the Magi.* Canvas.
Ca. 1640-1642. Guido Reni,
Italian. H. 367.3 cm. 69.132

*St. Catherine of Siena Receiving the Crown of
Thorns and a Rosary from the Christ Child.*
Canvas. Ca. 1643. Giovanni Battista Salvi
(called Sassoferrato), Italian. W. 83.8 cm.
66.332

138

Four Tondi: *Witches' Scenes.* Canvas. Ca. 1640. Salvator Rosa, Italian, 1615-1673.
D. 53.3 cm. (each). 77.37-.40

139

*The Feast of Terminus.* Red-brown oil. Giovanni Benedetto Castiglione, Italian, 1616-1670. W. 56.2 cm. 64.31

*Baptism of Christ.* Bronze. Ca. 1646. Alessandro Algardi, Italian, Rome. H. 62.3 cm. 65.471

*The Vision of St. Jerome.* Canvas. Giovanni Battista Langetti, Italian, Genoa, 1625-1676. H. 200.2 cm. 51.334

*Adoration of the Shepherds.* Canvas. Carlo Dolci, Italian, 1616-1686. H. 88.6 cm. 68.22

*The Apparition of the Virgin to St. Francis of Assisi.* Canvas. Ca. 1680-1683. Luca Giordano, Italian, Naples. H. 239 cm. 66.125

*The Risen Christ Appearing to His Mother.* Canvas. Ca. 1708. Francesco Solimena, Italian, Naples. H. 222.5 cm. 71.63

*Casket.* For Pietro Gregorio Boncompagni-Ludovisi and Maria Francesca Ottoboni. Silver gilt, malachite, lapis lazuli, and enamel. Italy, Rome, 1731. L. 22.8 cm. 74.86

141

*Education of the Virgin.* Marble.
Attr. to Giuseppe Mazzuoli, Italian,
1644-1725. H. 110.5 cm. 73.6

*The Rest on the Flight into Egypt.* Terra cotta.
Giuseppe Mazza, Italian, 1653-1741. H. 32.1 cm.
64.427

*Journey of a Patriarch.* Canvas. Giovanni Benedetto
Castiglione, Italian, 1616-1670. W. 78.4 cm. 69.1

*The Synagogue.* Canvas. Alessandro Magnasco,
Italian, Genoa, 1667-1749. W. 149 cm. 30.22

*David and Goliath.* Terra cotta. 1723. Giovanni
Battista Foggini, Italian, Florence. H. 41.3 cm.
66.126

*The Supper at Emmaus.* Canvas. Giovanni Battista
Piazzetta, Italian, Venice, 1682-1754. W. 141.3 cm.
31.245

*The Assumption of the Virgin.*
Painted 1744. Canvas (modello).
Giovanni Battista Piazzetta, Italian,
Venice. H. 71.5 cm. 55.165

*Il fiorellin d'amore (Little Flower of Love).* Black
chalk heightened with white chalk. Giovanni Battista
Piazzetta, Italian, 1682-1754. W. 54.9 cm. 38.387

143

Clockwise from upper left: *The Angels Appearing to Abraham, The Sacrifice of Isaac, Tobias and the Angel, Abraham Welcoming the Three Angels.* Canvas. Giovanni Antonio Guardi, Italian, Venice, 1698-1760. W. 75.5 cm. (each). 52.237, 52.235, 52.236, 52.238

*The Adoration of the Magi.* Pen and
bistre ink and bistre wash.
Giovanni Battista Tiepolo, Italian,
1696-1770. H. 38.7 cm. 44.474

*Horatius Cocles Defending Rome Against the Etruscans.*
Canvas. Giovanni Battista Tiepolo, Italian, Venice,
1696-1770. W. 208.3 cm. 49.571

*Martyrdom of St. Sebastian.*
Modello for the Diessen Altarpiece.
Canvas. Painted ca. 1739.
Giovanni Battista Tiepolo, Italian,
Venice. H. 52.8 cm. 46.277

*The Flight into Egypt: The Holy Family Embarking in a
Small Boat.* Pen and bistre ink and bistre wash.
Giovanni Battista Tiepolo, Italian, 1696-1770.
W. 44.6 cm. 29.443

145

*Interior of the Pantheon, Rome.* Dated 1747. Canvas.
Giovanni Paolo Panini, Italian. H. 125.7 cm. 74.39

*Portrait of a Lady.* Canvas.
Giovanni Domenico Tiepolo, Italian,
Venice, 1727-1804. H. 60.4 cm.
52.541

*The Spring Shower.* Pen and bistre ink and bistre wash.
Giovanni Domenico Tiepolo, Italian, 1727-1804.
W. 41.3 cm. 37.573

*The Prisons: An Immense Interior
with a Drawbridge.* Etching, state
I/III. Giovanni Battisti Piranesi,
Italian, 1720-1778. H. 54.8 cm.
41.30

146

*Visit of Pope Pius VI in Venice: The Reception of the Doge and Senate in the Salla delle Udienze in the Monastery of San Domenico.* Canvas. 1782. Francesco Guardi, Italian, Venice. W. 69 cm. 49.187

*Visit of Pope Pius VI in Venice: Te Deum in the Church of SS. Giovanni e Paolo.* Canvas. 1782. Francesco Guardi, Italian, Venice. W. 69 cm. 49.188

*A Procession of Triumphal Cars in Piazzo S. Marco, Venice.* Pen and bistre ink and bistre wash. 1782. Francesco Guardi, Italian. W. 36.7 cm. 55.164

*The Spring Shower.* Pen and bistre ink and bistre wash. Giovanni Domenico Tiepolo, Italian, 1727-1804. W. 41.3 cm. 37.573

*View of the Piazza San Marco, Venice, and the Piazzetta towards San Giorgio*
*Maggiore.* Canvas. Giovanni Antonio Canale (called Canaletto), Italian,
Venice, 1697-1768. W. 232.5 cm.  62.169

*Views of Venice and Environs: The Tower of Malghera.*
Etching, state I/II. Giovanni Antonio Canale (called
Canaletto), Italian, 1697-1768. W. 43.4 cm.  25.1240

*Imaginary View: A Palace on the Shore of the Lagoon.*
Pen and brown ink with gray wash. Giovanni Antonio
Canale (called Canaletto), Italian, 1697-1768.
W. 42.1 cm.  30.23

148

*Pietà.* Canvas. Painted after 1750. Giuseppe
Bazzani, Italian. W. 141.7 cm.  55.682

*Woman and Man.* Soft paste
porcelain. Italy, Naples, Caop-di-
Monte, ca. 1750. H. 18.4 cm.
50.569

*Standing Woman.* Soft paste
porcelain. Italy, Naples, Capo-di-
Monte, ca. 1750. H. 20.3 cm.
50.570

149

*The Holy Family.* Canvas. El Greco (Domenico Theotocópuli), Spanish, 1541-1614. H. 131.7 cm. 26.247

*Portrait of the Jester Calabazas.* Canvas. Diego Rodriguez de Silva y Velázquez, Spanish, 1599-1660. H. 175 cm. 65.15

*Christ on the Cross with Landscape.* Canvas. El Greco (Domenico Theotocópuli), Spanish, 1541-1614. H. 188 cm. 52.222

*The Holy House of Nazareth.* Canvas. Francisco de Zurbarán, Spanish, 1598-1662/64. W. 218 cm. 60.117

*The Virgin and Child.* Pen and brown ink, ink wash, red and black chalk. Ca. 1670. Bartolomé Esteban Murillo, Spanish. H. 21.4 cm. 68.66

*Laban Searching for His Stolen Household Gods in Rachel's Tent.* Canvas. Bartolomé Estéban Murillo, Spanish, 1618-1682. W. 363.9 cm. 65.469

*The Immaculate Conception.* Canvas. Bartolomé Estéban Murillo, Spanish, 1618-1682. H. 220.5 cm. 59.189

*The Death of Adonis.* Canvas. Jusepe de Ribera, Spanish, 1591-1652.
W. 238.8 cm. 65.19

*St. Jerome.* Canvas. Jusepe de Ribera, Spanish, 1591-
1652. H. 129 cm. 61.219

*Portrait of the Infante Don Luis de Borbón.* Canvas. Painted 1783. Francisco José de Goya y Lucientes, Spanish. H. 152.7 cm. 66.14

*Portrait of Don Juan Antonio Cuervo.* Dated 1819. Canvas. Francisco José de Goya y Lucientes, Spanish. H. 120 cm. 43.90

*St. Ambrose.* Canvas. Francisco José de Goya y Lucientes, Spanish, 1746-1828. H. 190 cm. 69.23

*The Bulls of Bordeaux: The Celebrated American, Mariano Ceballos.* Lithograph, state II/II. Francisco de Goya y Lucientes, Spanish, 1746-1828. W. 40.4 cm. 49.2

*The Garroted Man.* Etching, state I/II. Francisco de Goya y Lucientes, Spanish, 1746-1828. H. 32.8 cm. 63.470

153

*Hercules and Cacus.* Dated 1588.
Chiaroscuro woodcut. Hendrik
Goltzius, Dutch. H. 41 cm.
75.60

*Samson and Delilah.* Canvas. Ca. 1618-1620. Gerrit
van Honthorst, Dutch, Utrecht. H. 129 cm.  68.23

*The Weeping Heraclitus.* Dated 1621.
Canvas. Hendrick Terbrugghen,
Dutch. H. 125 cm.  77.2

*Portrait of Isabella Brant.* Panel.
Ca. 1622. Peter Paul Rubens, Flemish.
H. 53 cm.  47.207

*The Feast of Herod.* Pen and bistre ink with charcoal
and red chalk. Ca. 1630-1640. Peter Paul Rubens,
Flemish. W. 47.3 cm.  54.2

*A Genoese Lady with Her Child.* Canvas. Ca. 1627.
Sir Anthony van Dyck, Flemish. H. 217.8 cm.  54.392

*Diana and Her Nymphs Departing for the Chase.*
Canvas. Ca. 1615. Peter Paul Rubens, Flemish.
H. 215.9 cm.  59.190

155

*The Betrayal of Christ.* Canvas. Jacob Jordaens, Flemish, Antwerp, 1593-1678. W. 246.3 cm. 70.32

*Pastoral Scene.* Canvas. Jan Siberechts, Flemish, 1627-1703. W. 122.5 cm. 69.18

*Peasants Drinking and Smoking.* Panel. David Teniers the Younger, Flemish, 1610-1690. H. 37.2 cm. 16.1046

*The Conversion of St. Paul with Horseman and Banner.* Ink, black and red chalk, and water color. Ca. 1645. Jacob Jordaens, Flemish. H. 32.8 cm. 54.366

*A View of Emmerich Across the Rhine.* Dated 1645.
Panel. Jan van Goyen, Dutch. W. 95.3 cm. 59.351

*Wooded Landscape with Sleeping Peasants.* Dated 165(0?).
Canvas. Simon de Vlieger, Dutch. W. 130.4 cm. 75.76

*Landscape with a Cottage and Figures.*
Dated 1653. Pencil and gray wash.
Jan van Goyen, Dutch. W. 27.5 cm.
29.548

*Dune Landscape with Figures.* Panel.
Philips Wouwerman, Dutch, 1619-1668.
W. 41.5 cm. 67.124

*View of Orleans on the Loire.* Pen
and brown ink, brown and gray wash.
Lambert Doomer, Dutch, 1622/23-1700.
W. 41.1 cm. 66.4

*Portrait of a Lady in a Ruff.*
Dated 1638. Canvas. Frans Hals,
Dutch. H. 69.7 cm. 48.137

*Hilly Landscape with Hut Beside a
Stream.* Dated 1627. Black chalk
and tan and gray wash. Esaias van
de Velde, Dutch. W. 29.2 cm. 66.7

*Protestant Gothic Church with Motifs
of the Oude Kerk in Amsterdam.*
Canvas. Emanuel de Witte, Dutch,
Alkmaar, 1617-1692. H. 62 cm.
71.1

*River Landscape with Castle.* Dated 1644. Panel.
Salomon van Ruysdael, Dutch. W. 60.6 cm. 73.2

*Fishing Boats in a Harbor.* Canvas. Allart van
Everdingen, Dutch, 1621-1675. W. 97 cm. 74.105

*Portrait of a Youth.* Dated 1632. Panel. Rembrandt Harmensz van Rijn, Dutch. H. 57.8 cm. 42.644

*Portrait of a Lady.* Dated 1635. Panel. Rembrandt Harmensz van Rijn, Dutch. H. 77.5 cm. 44.90

*Portrait of a Jewish Student.* Canvas. Rembrandt Harmensz van Rijn, Dutch, 1606-1669. H. 84.5 cm. 50.252

*Christ Taken Before Caiaphas.* Pen, reed pen, and brush with bistre ink and touches of white. Ca. 1641-1642. Rembrandt Harmensz van Rijn, Dutch. W. 23.4 cm. 60.187

*Tobias Healing His Father's Blindness.* Pen and brown ink corrected with white wash. Rembrandt Harmensz van Rijn, Dutch, 1606-1669. W. 21.1 cm. 69.69

159

*Old Man with a Flowing Beard.* Dated
1631. Etching, state I/II. Rembrandt
Harmensz van Rijn, Dutch. H. 6.8 cm.
73.38

*Old Man Praying.* Dated 166(1?). Canvas. Rembrandt
Harmensz van Rijn, Dutch. H. 87.6 cm.  67.16

*The Three Trees.* Etching and drypoint. 1643.
Rembrandt Harmensz van Rijn, Dutch. W. 21.3 cm.  66.334

*Christ Preaching (La Petite Tombe).* Etching. Rembrandt
Harmensz van Rijn, Dutch, 1606-1669. W. 20.8 cm.  58.306

160

*The Three Crosses.* Dated 1653. Etching and drypoint, state IV/V. Rembrandt Harmensz van Rijn, Dutch. W. 44.2 cm.  59.241

*Still Life.* Dated 1663. Canvas. Willem Kalf, Dutch. H. 60.4 cm.  62.292

*Landscape with a Windmill.* Dated 1646. Panel. Jacob van Ruisdael, Dutch. W. 68.5 cm.  67.19

*The Meeting of Christ with Martha and Mary after the Death of Lazarus.* Reed pen and bistre with touches of white. Ca. 1662-1665. Rembrandt Harmensz van Rijn, Dutch. W. 20.8 cm.  62.116

161

*View of the Heerengracht, Amsterdam.* Canvas.
Ca. 1660-1662. Jan Wijnants, Dutch. W. 81.9 cm.
64.419

*Travelers in a Hilly Landscape with a River.*
Panel. Ca. 1650-1655. Aelbert Cuyp, Dutch.
W. 74.8 cm. 42.637

*Landscape with a Dead Tree.* Canvas. Ca. 1665-1668.
Jacob van Ruisdael, Dutch. W. 131 cm. 67.63

*A Wooded and Hilly Landscape, Evening.* Canvas.
Ca. 1663-1665. Jacob van Ruisdael, Dutch. W. 59.4 cm.
63.575

162

*Portrait of a Standing Lady.* Canvas. Gerard ter Borch (Terborch), Dutch, 1617-1681. H. 63.3 cm. 44.93

*Esther, Ahasuerus and Haman.* Canvas. Ca. 1667-1669. Jan Steen, Dutch. W. 92.9 cm. 64.153

*A Music Party.* Dated 1663. Canvas. Pieter de Hooch, Dutch. W. 119.4 cm. 51.355

*Landscape with Sleeping Shepherdess.* Dated 1663. Panel. Adriaen van der Velde, Dutch. W. 27.5 cm. 66.12

163

*Mountainous Landscape.* Pencil and ink. Nicolas
Berchem, Dutch, 1620-1683. W. 52.0 cm. 58.410

*A Wooded Landscape with Figures.* Canvas. Meindert
Hobbema, Dutch, 1638-1709. W. 111.8 cm. 42.641

164

*The Descent from the Cross.* Ivory.
Dated 1653. Adam Lenckhardt,
Austrian. H. 44.4 cm. 67.134

*Covered Cup.* Silver and silver
gilt. 1688. Johann Andreas Thelot,
German, Augsburg. H. 40 cm.
66.111

*Pilgrim Bottle.* Polished stoneware
with silver-gilt mounts. Germany,
Meissen, ca. 1715. H. 15.9 cm.
51.451

*Covered Goblet.* Engraved glass.
Bohemia, ca. 1715. H. 47.9 cm.
50.390

*Goblet.* Engraved glass. 1680.
Herman Schwinger, German, Nuremberg.
H. 31.1 cm. 50.389

*Tankard.* Silver, partially gilt.
Andreas Brachfeldt, Russian, Riga,
late 17th century. *Relief.* Silver.
Master D. M., German, Augsburg,
H. 25.3 cm. 71.266

165

*Sacred and Profane Love.* Chasuble. Embroidery, silk and metallic threads on silk. Bavaria, 4th quarter 17th century. Over-all: H. 116 cm. Detail: H. 43.5 cm. 71.235

*Christ at the Column.* Gilt bronze. Dated 1756. Johann Baptist Hagenauer, Austrian. H. 19.1 cm. 53.286

*God the Father.* Polychromed wood. Johann Peter Schwanthaler the Elder, Austrian, 1720-1795. H. 141.6 cm. 61.30

*St. Joachim.* Gilded wood. Joseph Anton Feuchtmeyer (or his circle), South German, 1696-1770. H. 128.9 cm. 62.246

*House Altarpiece.* Carved and gilded wood. Ca. 1740. Joseph Matthias Götz, German, Bavarià. H. 165.1 cm. 64.357

*Return from the Flight into Egypt.* Canvas. Josef
Ignaz Mildorfer, Austrian, 1719-1775. H. 118 cm. 74.2

*Presentation of Christ in the Temple.* Canvas.
Painted ca. 1750/55. Franz Anton Maulbertsch,
Austrian. H. 69.5 cm. 63.326

*Madonna of the Immaculate
Conception.* Painted and gilded wood.
Ca. 1770. Franz Ignaz Gunther,
German. H. 77.5 cm. 63.294

*Kneeling Angel.* Carved wood. Ca.
1760. Franz Ignaz Gunther, German,
1725-1775. H. 79.7 cm. 66.18

*Male Figure.* Wood. Ca. 1760.
Franz Ignaz Gunther, German.
H. 95 cm. 73.101

*Kneeling Saint.* Painted wood. Ca. 1740-1750. Johann Baptist Straub, German, Munich. H. 118.1 cm. 61.414

*Orpheus.* Stone. Ca. 1765. Ferdinand Tietz, German. H. 183 cm. 71.65

*Spring.* Painted wood. Ca. 1765. Ferdinand Tietz, German. H. 14 cm. 62.209

*Console Table.* Made for Schloss Seehof, Franconia. Carved and gilded wood. Ca. 1765. Attr. to Ferdinand Tietz, German. H. 85.7 cm. 62.63

*Clock.* Carved and gilded wood. Faience. Ca. 1750. Works by Baumgartinger, Mergentheim, Germany. H. 97.8 cm. 66.362

168

*Pluto.* Porcelain. Ca. 1760.
Modeled by Franz Anton Bustelli,
German, Munich, Nymphenburg Factory.
H. 10.2 cm. 47.283

*Box.* Gold and mother-of-pearl.
Austria, Vienna (?), ca. 1765.
H. 9.2 cm. 67.157

*Gilt-Bronze Dish.* Germany (?), 2nd
quarter 18th century. H. 31.9 cm.
55.69

*Count Tschernitscheff, Russian
Ambassador at Vienna.* Ivory.
Friedrich Heinrich Füger, Germany,
1751-1818. D. 10.1 cm. 42.1141

*Portrait of a Lady.* Dated 1619. Panel. Cornelius I. Johnson, English. H. 65.7 cm. 73.185

*Portrait of a Lady of the Earle Family.* Canvas. Sir Peter Lely, English, 1618-1680. H. 126.7 cm. 42.247

*Story of David and Bathsheba.* Dated 1658. Stumpwork embroidery: silk and metallic yarns, pearls and carved wood appendages, on silk. England. W. 53.3 cm. 73.186

*King Henry VIII Treading on the Pope.* Panel of petit-point embroidery, silk. England, Period of Charles I (1625-1648). W. 55.3 cm. 19.585

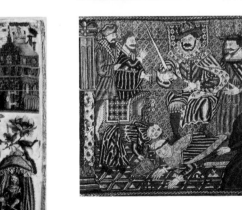

*Armchair.* Walnut with caned back.
England, ca. 1680-1685. H. 38.1 cm.
42.573

*Covered Cup.* Silver and silver gilt.
1677-1678. I. A. (unidentified),
English, London. H. 17.2 cm. 58.422

*Knife, Fork, and Spoon.* Gold.
Germany, Augsburg, ca. 1725.
L. 19.1, 19.1, and 22.2 cm.
63.473-63.475

*Covered Cup.* Silver. 1686-1687.
W. I. (unidentified), English,
London. H. 23.8 cm. 35.145

171

*Charles II, King of England.* 1653. Canvas. Philippe de Champaigne, French. H. 125.7 cm. 59.38

*The Dance of the Boys and Girls.* Canvas. Mathieu Le Nain, French, 1607-1677. W. 120.5 cm. 57.489

*Samson.* Canvas. 1630/31. Valentin de Boulogne, French. H. 135.6 cm. 72.50

*The Repentant St. Peter.* Dated 1645. Canvas. Georges de la Tour, French. H. 114.5 cm. 51.454

172

*Italian Landscape.* Dated 163(?). Canvas. Claude Gellée (called Claude Lorrain), French. W. 137 cm. 46.73

*Landscape with Hunting Figures.* Canvas. Gaspard Dughet, French, 1615-1675. W. 175.2 cm. 70.30

*Landscape with Cattle.* Pen and brown ink and ink wash. Claude Gellée (called Claude Lorrain), French, 1600-1682. W. 40.1 cm. 28.15

*Landscape with Rest on the Flight into Egypt.* Canvas. Claude Gellée (called Claude Lorrain), French, 1600-1682. H. 205 cm. 62.151

173

*Head of a Philosopher.* Marble.
Dated 1662. Pierre Puget, French.
H. 39.4 cm. 69.121

*The Blessed Alessandro Sauli.*
Terra cotta. Ca. 1665-1667.
Pierre Puget, French. H. 69.7 cm.
64.36

*The Tree of Christ.* Black chalk.
Laurent de la Hyre, French, 1606/16-
1656/8. W. 46.4 cm. 72.98

*The Kiss of Peace and Justice.* 1654. Canvas. Laurent
de la Hyre, French. W. 76.2 cm. 71.102

*Rest on the Flight into Egypt.* Panel. Simon Vouet,
French, 1590-1649. W. 45.7 cm. 73.32

174

*Ebony Cabinet.* Wood, metal, and tortoise shell. Ca. 1690. Attr. to André-Charles Boulle, French, Paris. H. 101.3 cm. 49.539

*Gaming Table.* Wood and ivory marquetry. Northern Italy or Southern Germany, ca. 1730. H. 77.7 cm. 53.284

*Pier Glass with Frame (Trumeau).* Carved and gilded wood. France, ca. 1715. H. approx. 242.8 cm. 53.153

*Armchair.* Oak. France, ca. 1715-1725. H. 116.8 cm. 25.1219

*Clock.* Tortoise shell and brass inlay, gilt bronze. Ca. 1695. André-Charles Boulle, French, Paris. H. 113.7 cm. 67.153

*Vase.* Soft paste porcelain. France, Rouen, Poterat Factory (?), ca. 1680. H. 21.6 cm. 47.63

*Study for the Romancer.* Red and black chalk. Jean Antoine Watteau, French, 1684-1721. H. 35 cm. 28.661

*Portrait of Cardinal Dubois.* Dated 1723. Canvas. Hyacinthe Rigaud, French. H. 146.7 cm. 67.17

*The Elements: Air.* Tapestry, silk, wool, and cotton. France, Paris, Gobelin Factory, 18th century. H. 353 cm. 42.495

*Spring.* Savonnerie panel, Ghiordes knot, silk and wool. France, Paris, Savonnerie Factory, 18th century. H. 139.8 cm. 52.14

*The Swing.* Canvas. Nicolas Lancret, French, 1690-1743. H. 151.1 cm. 48.180

176

*The Minuet in a Pavilion.* Canvas.
Jean Baptiste Pater, French, 1695-
1736. H. 55.3 cm. 38.392

*Seated Chinese with Pot.* Soft paste
porcelain. France, Chantilly, ca.
1740. H. 17.2 cm. 47.62

*Cachepot.* Soft paste porcelain.
France, Paris, Villeroy Factory,
ca. 1735-1740. D. 19.4 cm. 47.60

*Pan and Syrinx.* Dated 1720. Canvas. Jean-François de
Troy, French. W. 139 cm. 73.212

*Portrait of Anne Louis Goislard de Montsabert,
Comte de Richebourg-le Toureil.* Dated 1734.
Canvas. Nicolas de Largillierre, French.
H. 80.7 cm. 70.31

*Portrait of Jean-Gabriel de la Porte du Theil.*
Canvas. Ca. 1739/40. Jacques-André-Joseph-Camelot
Aved, French. H. 124.5 cm. 64.89

*Cupids in Conspiracy.* Canvas. François Boucher,
French, 1703-1770. W. 123.8 cm. 48.182

*The Fountain.* Red, black, and white
chalk. François Boucher, French,
1703-1770. H. 38.1 cm. 52.529

*Tureen.* Silver. 1735-1738. Juste-Aurèle Meissonnier, French.
L. (tureen) 35 cm., (stand) 45 cm. 77.182

178

*Still Life with Herrings.* Canvas.
Jean-Baptiste Siméon Chardin, French,
1699-1779. H. 41 cm. 74.1

*Hare and Leg of Lamb.* Dated 1742. Canvas. Jean-
Baptiste Oudry, French. H. 73.4 cm. 69.53

*The Flute Player.* Tapestry, silk and wool. France,
Beauvais, 18th century. Design by François Boucher,
1755. H. 363.5 cm. 42.822

*Chinese Fair.* Tapestry, silk and wool. France,
Beauvais, 18th century. Design by François Boucher,
1743; cartoon by Jean Joseph Dumont. H. 322.8 cm.
44.134

179

*Mlle. De Savigny.* Canvas. Ca. 1748.
Jean Marc Nattier, French.
H. 81.9 cm. 48.183

*Madame de Pompadour as Diana.*
Dated 1752. Canvas. Jean Marc
Nattier, French. H. 100.4 cm.
42.643

*La Marquise d'Aiguirandes.* Dated
1759. Canvas. François Hubert
Drouais, French. H. 101 cm.
42.638

*Carpet.* Wool. France, Paris, Savonnerie Factory,
ca. 1750. H. 6 m. 10 cm. 50.8

180

*Microscope.* Gilt bronze. France, mid-18th century. H. 27.9 cm. 74.15

*Gilt Bronze Clock.* France, ca. 1750. H. 93 cm. 51.550

*Wall Clock.* Gilt bronze. France, ca. 1750-1760. H. 116.8 cm. 50.376

*Tall Clock (Regulateur).* Boulle marquetry with gilt bronze mounts. 1744. Jacques-Pierre Latz, French Paris. H. 261.5 cm. 49.200

*Commode.* Oak, tulipwood marquetry with gilt bronze mounts. Ca. 1750. Attr. to Jacques-Pierre Latz, French, Paris. H. 156.5 cm. 42.497

*Pair of Fire Dogs.* Gilt bronze. 1752. Jacques Caffieri, French, Paris. H. 44.2 cm. 42.799, 42.800

*Porcelain Vase.* Germany, Meissen, 1749. Gilt bronze mounts: France, Paris, ca. 1750. H. 31.1 cm. 44.230

*Pair of Parrots.* Porcelain. Ca. 1740. Modeled by Johann Joachim Kaendler, German, Meissen. *Pair of Candelabra.* Gilt bronze. France, Paris, ca. 1750. H. 18.9 cm. 38.305-38.308

182

*Monkey on a Dog.* Soft-paste
porcelain. France, Mennecy,
mid-18th century. H. 15.9 cm.
53.269

*Covered Bowl.* Soft paste porcelain.
France, Vincennes, ca. 1745.
H. 15.3 cm.  44.225

*Tureen.* Soft paste porcelain.
France, Vincennes, ca. 1752.
H. 25.7 cm.  52.3

*Bust of a Woman.* Terra cotta.
Jean Baptiste Lemoyne II, French,
1704-1778. H. 63.5 cm.  52.566

*Laban Cherchant ses Dieux.* Canvas. Ca. 1753.
Gabriel de Saint-Aubin, French. W. 55 cm.
65.548

183

*Fête in a Park with Costumed Dancers.* Ink, ink and
water-color washes, over pencil indications. Ca. 1760-
1765. Gabriel de Saint-Aubin, French. W. 31.3 cm.
66.124

*Six Miniatures.* Gouache on card.
1753. Louis Nicholas van Blarnberghe,
French. *Box.* Gold. 1753-1754. Jean
Charles Ducrollay, French, Paris.
H. 3.4 cm.  57.412

*Candelabrum.* Gilt bronze. Attr.
to Jean Joseph de Saint-Germain,
French, Paris, 1720-1791.
H. 72.4 cm.  46.81

*Candelabrum.* Silver. 1758.
François Thomas Germain, French,
Paris. H. 38.1 cm.  40.14

*Cachepot.* Faience. France,
Marseilles, Robert Factory, ca.
1765. H. 17.8 cm.  62.379

*Tureen.* Soft paste porcelain. France, Vincennes-Sèvres, 1756. H. 24.2 cm. 49.15

*Tureen with Platter.* Soft paste porcelain. France, Sèvres, 1757. Tureen: H. 24.2 cm. Platter: L. 40.6 cm. 53.25

*Covered Bowl.* Faience. France, Saint-Clément, ca. 1775. H. 13.4 cm. 61.2

*Tureen.* Faience. France, Strasbourg, ca. 1750. Tureen: H. 21.2 cm. Platter: L. 38.6 cm. 76.52

*Table-Desk (Bureau Plat).* Wood marquetry with gilt bronze mounts. Ca. 1750. Bernard van Risen Burgh II, French, Paris. H. 74.9 cm. 44.123

*Table-Desk (Bureau Plat).* Wood marquetry with gilt bronze mounts. Ca. 1750. Jacques Dubois, French, Paris. H. 80 cm. 42.591

*Straw Marquetry Desk.* France, 3rd quarter 18th century. H. 97.2 cm. 42.40

186

*Morpheus or Allegory of Sleep.* Canvas. France, 18th century. W. 130 cm. 63.502

*Young Boy Dressed in a Red-Lined Cloak* (The Artist's Son?). Canvas. Ca. 1789. Jean Honoré Fragonard, French. H. 21 cm. 42.49

*Roman Ruins, Villa Pamfili.* Dated 1774. Pen and brown ink; blue, gray, and red-brown water color. Hubert Robert, French. W. 44.5 cm. 51.485

*Invocation to Love.* Pen and brown ink and ink wash. Jean Honoré Fragonard, French, 1732-1806. W. 41.6 cm. 43.657

*The Grotto of Posillipo with Imaginary Architecture.*
Canvas. Ca. 1769. Hubert Robert, French. H. 109.2 cm.
76.98

*Interior of the Colonnade of St. Peter's at the Time
of the Conclave.* Canvas. Ca. 1769. Hubert Robert,
French. H. 109.2 cm. 76.97

*Landscape with Shepherds.* Pastel and gouache on prepared
fabric. Dated 1779. Jean Pillement, French. W. 61 cm.
73.1

*View of Rome.* Paper mounted on pulpboard. Pierre
Henri de Valenciennes, French, 1750-1819. W. 38.9 cm.
70.55

188

*Textile Panel.* Lampas weave, brocaded and embroidered, silk. France, Lyon, design by Jean Démosthène Dugourc, ca. 1790. Over-all: H. 237 cm. Detail: H. 131 cm. 35.237

*Young Girl.* Terra cotta. Claude Michel (called Clodion), French, 1738-1814. H. 45.1 cm. 42.50

*Satyress and Child.* Terra cotta. 1803. Claude Michel (called Clodion), French. D. 30.8 cm. 63.251

*Chest of Drawers with Panels of Oriental Lacquer.* Ebony veneer. Japanese lacquer panels, gilt-bronze mounts. René Dubois, French, Paris, 1737-1799. H. 86.9 cm. 44.113

*Armchair* (one of a pair). Carved and gilded wood. Jacques-Jean-Baptiste Tilliard (called Jean Baptiste II Tilliard), French, Paris, active 1752-1797. H. 102.5 cm. 27.424

*Candelabrum.* Bronze and gilt bronze with marble base. Ca. 1785. Claude Michel, called Clodion, French. H. 160.3 cm. 44.125

*Candelabrum.* Bronze, gilt bronze, and gray marble. Ca. 1785. Claude Michel, called Clodion, French. H. 92.1 cm. 42.59

*Fire Dog* (one of a pair). Gilt bronze. France, ca. 1785. H. 46.3 cm. 44.126

*Table.* Mahogany, with gilt-bronze mounts and white marble top. Ca. 1785. Adam Weisweiler, French, Paris. H. 91.5 cm. 22.73

*Boudoir from the Hotel d'Hocqueville.* Carved and painted wood with plaster ceiling and ornamental reliefs. Ca. 1785. France, Rouen. H. 4.09 m. 70.53

*Work Table.* Wood marquetry with
gilt-bronze mounts. Sèvres porcelain
top. Martin Carlin, French, Paris,
active 1766-1785. H. 77.5 cm. 42.594

*Six Miniatures Mounted in Oval Box.*
Gouache miniatures mounted in gold
and enamel. Dated 1779-1780 (?).
Pierre Marie Gault de Saint-Germain,
French, Paris. H. 3.4 cm. 57.409

*Armchair* (one of a pair). Carved
and partially gilded boxwood.
Nicholas-Denis Delaisement, French,
Paris, act. 1776-after 1792.
H. 98.1 cm. 44.110

*Stool.* Made for Marie Antoinette's
game room at Compiègne, but used at
Fontainbleu. Carved and gilded wood.
1786-1787. Jean-Baptiste-Claude Sené,
French, Paris. H. 44.7 cm. 54.385

*Chair* (one of a set of four).
Carved, painted and gilded wood with
Beauvais tapestry covers. Ca. 1780.
Georges Jacob, French, Paris.
H. 90.5 cm. 42.75

*Tureen and Platter.* Silver. 1798-1809. Henri
Auguste, French, Paris. Tureen: H. 26.2 cm.
Platter: D. 49.2 cm. 52.592

*Ecuelle.* Porcelain. France, Sèvres, 1795, decorations
by Dodin (1734-1802). Plate: D. 23.5 cm.
Bowl: D. 19.5 cm. 71.64

*Small Writing Table.* Wood marquetry
with gilt-bronze mounts. Jean-
Francois Leleu, French, Paris,
active 1764-1792. H. 73.7 cm.
44.115

*Armchair* (one of a set). Carved and
painted wood, covered in Aubusson
tapestry after a design by Huet.
Ca. 1785. Henri Jacob, French,
Paris. H. 96.5 cm. 42.30

*Rectangular Box.* Enamel on gold.
France, Paris, 1768-1769 (?).
H. 4.5 cm. 57.410

192

*Monteith.* Silver gilt. Dated 1715-1716. Benjamin
Pyne, English. H. 27 cm.  65.467

*The Ladies Amabel and Mary Jemima Yorke.* Canvas.
Painted 1761. Sir Joshua Reynolds, English.
H. 195.5 cm.  42.645

*Tea Caddy.* Silver gilt. 1741-1742.
Paul de Lamerie, English, London.
H. 13.3 cm.  43.179

*Punch Bowl.* Soft paste porcelain. England, Worcester,
ca. 1770. D. 27.6 cm.  38.331

193

*Study for the Portrait of Mrs. Sarah Siddons.* Black chalk. Thomas Gainsborough, English, 1727-1788. H. 46.6 cm. 76.6

*Scene with a Road Winding Through a Wood.* Pen and brown ink and gray wash. Thomas Gainsborough, English, 1727-1788. W. 25.1 cm. 29.547

*George Pitt, First Lord Rivers (1721-1803).* Canvas. Painted late 1768 or early 1769. Thomas Gainsborough, English. H. 234.3 cm. 71.2

194

*Young Man in Blue.* Dated 1778.
On Ivory. John Smart, English.
H. 3.5 cm. 40.1219

*Woman Standing Among the Friars.* Pencil and ink washes.
John Brown, Scottish, 1752-1787. W. 36.9 cm. 69.28

*A Storm Behind the Isle of Wight.* Canvas. Julius
Caesar Ibbetson, English, 1759-1817. W. 67.5 cm.
48.461

195

*Marble Mantel.* England, late 18th century.
H. 152.4 cm. 44.471

*Centerpiece.* Silver. 1808-1809. Paul Storr, English,
London. H. 66.1 cm. 43.189

*Lady Louisa Manners, later Countess
of Dysart, as Juno.* Canvas. Sir
Thomas Lawrence, English, 1769-
1830. H. 255.3 cm. 61.220

*General Duncan Campbell.* Canvas.
Ca. 1806. Sir Henry Raeburn,
English. H. 76.2 cm. 47.266

*The Daughters of Colonel Thomas
Carteret Hardy.* Canvas. Painted
1801. Sir Thomas Lawrence, English.
H. 129 cm. 42.642

196

*Teapot.* Silver. Nathaniel Hurd, American, Boston, 1729-1777. H. 14.6 cm. 40.228

*Spoon.* Silver. 1661. John Hull and Robert Sanderson, American, Boston. L. 15.9 cm. 40.214

*Tankard.* Silver. Edward Winslow, American, Boston, 1669-1753. H. 19 cm. 40.283

*Brazier.* Silver with wood handle and feet. John Potwine, American, Boston, 1698-1792. H. 8.2 cm. 40.248

*Portrait of Charles Apthorp.* Dated 1748. Canvas.
Robert Feke, American, ca. 1705-ca. 1750. H. 127 cm.
19.1006

*Portrait of Mrs. Thomas Bulfinch.*
Canvas. Ca. 1733. John Smibert,
American. H. 75.5 cm. 3919.20

*Plate.* From a service made for Samuel Shaw. Porcelain.
Ca. 1790. China, made for the American market.
D. 19.7 cm. 61.178

*Portrait of Nathaniel Hurd.* Canvas. Ca. 1765.
John Singleton Copley, American. H. 76.2 cm. 15.534

*Portrait of Mrs. John Greene.* Dated 1769. Canvas.
John Singleton Copley, American. H. 125.5 cm. 15.527

*Mrs. West and Her Son Raphael.* Canvas. Ca. 1770.
Benjamin West, American. W. 89.5 cm. 27.393

*A Hussar Officer on Horseback.*
Black and white chalk on blue paper.
John Singleton Copley, American,
1737-1815. H. 27.5 cm. 50.216

199

*Portrait of George Washington.* Canvas. Ca. 1790.
Joseph Wright, American. H. 53.3 cm.  2553.21

*George Washington at the Battle of Princeton.* Canvas.
Ca. 1779-1780. Charles Willson Peale, American.
H. 132 cm.  17.946

*Portrait of Mrs. John Thomson
Mason.* Canvas. Ca. 1803. Gilbert
Stuart, American. H. 72.4 cm.
21.428

*Plate.* From a service made for Samuel Shaw. Porcelain.
Ca. 1790. China, made for the American market.
D. 19.7 cm.  61.178

*Captain Jean T. David.* Dated 1813. Canvas. Thomas Sully, American. H. 89.5 cm. 16.1979

*Portrait of Samuel Williams.* Canvas. Ca. 1818. Washington Allston, American. H. 142.2 cm. 65.474

*Chair.* From a set of furniture made for the Derby family, Salem. Carved mahogany with ebony feet. Attr. to Samuel McIntire, American, Salem, 1757-1811. H. 97.1 cm. 62.125

*Pair of Spurs.* Silver. Paul Revere, Jr., American, Boston, 1735-1818. W. 11.4 cm. 40.252, 40.253

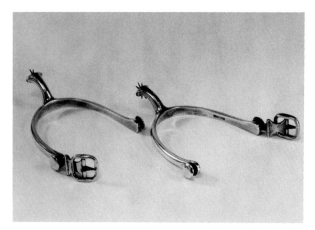

*Sofa.* Wood. America, New York, Empire Style, ca. 1820. L. 195.6 cm.
71.29

*Front Doorway.* From the Isaac Gillet House, Painesville,
Ohio. Carved and painted wood, glass, and metal.
Designed by Jonathon Goldsmith, American, Ohio, 1783-
1847. H. approx. 292.5 cm.  59.342

202

*Cupid and Psyche.* Dated 1817. Canvas. Jacques Louis David, French. W. 241.6 cm. 62.37

*Madame Dugazon as Andromache.* Canvas. Ca. 1783. Jacques Louis David, French. H. 52 cm. 52.542

Lateral panels for the "Bataille des Pyramides": *General Kléber* (left) and *Native Family* (right). Canvas. Baron Antoine-Jean Gros, French, 1771-1835. H. 304.8 cm. each. 72.17, 72.18

*Self-Portrait.* Canvas. Louis-Lie Perin-Salbreux, French, 1753-1817. H. 63.2 cm. 61.334

203

*Portrait of Comte Jean-Antoine Chaptal.* Canvas. Dated 1824. Baron Antoine-Jean Gros, French. H. 136.5 cm. 64.54

*Study of a Nude Woman, Seated Looking to the Right.* Black and white chalk on blue paper. Pierre Paul Prud'hon, French, 1758-1823. H. 61.9 cm. 61.318

*Fowling Piece* (detail). Steel, partially gilt, silver, walnut. Ca. 1809. Le Page, French, Paris. Total L. 116.5 cm. 66.433

*Flower Stand.* Wood and gilt bronze. Ca. 1800. Mounts made by Pierre Philippe Thomire, French. H. 104.2 cm. 60.94

*Terpsichore.* Marble. Dated 1816. Antonio Canova, Italian. H. 177.5 cm. 68.212

*Portrait of Madame Raoul-Rochette.*
Dated 1830. Pencil. Jean Auguste
Dominique Ingres, French.
H. 32.2 cm. 27.437

*Odalisque.* Canvas. France, 19th century. W. 92 cm.
39.63

*Antiochus and Stratonice.* Canvas. Painted 1834.
Jean Auguste Dominique Ingres, French. W. 63.5 cm.
66.13

*Pasture Rose (Rosa Carolina
Corymbosa).* Water color on vellum.
Pierre Joseph Redouté, French,
1759-1840. H. 39.1 cm. 59.15

*Greek Pirates Attacking a Turkish Vessel.* Dated 1827.
Canvas. Eugène Louis Gabriel Isabey, French. W. 74.2 cm.
16.1034

*Portrait of Comte Palatiano in the Costume of a
Palikare.* Canvas. Ca. 1826 or 1827. Eugène Delacroix,
French. H. 40.7 cm. 73.33

*Mlle. Julie de la Boutraye.*
Canvas. 1834. Eugène Delacroix,
French. H. 73 cm. 62.3

*The Curious One (Le Curieux).* Paper on canvas.
Dated 1823. Antoine-Pierre Mongin, French.
H. 43.5 cm. 77.116

*Halt of the Greek Cavaliers.* Dated 1858. Canvas.
Eugène Delacroix, French. W. 61 cm. 16.1032

*Armored Figure on Horseback.* Pencil and sepia wash.
Eugène Delacroix, French, 1798-1863. W. 39.8 cm. 33.418

*Fighting Horses.* Pencil and brown, blue, and black
washes. Théodore Géricault, French, 1791-1824.
W. 29.5 cm. 29.13

*Wild Horse.* Dated 1828. Lithograph,
state I/II. Eugène Delacroix, French.
H. 34.3 cm. 41.214

207

*The Roman Campagna.* Canvas. 1826/27. Jean Baptiste Camille Corot. French. W. 135.2 cm. 63.91

*Duchess of Ragusa.* Dated 1818. On vellum. Jean-Baptiste Isabey, French. H. 12.7 cm. 42.1146

*Return from the Fields.* Canvas. Jean-François Millet, French, 1814-1875. H. 45.7 cm. 72.19

*Landscape with Satyr.* Canvas. Dated 1841. Célestin Nanteuil, French. W. 130.5 cm. 77.125

*Burning of the Houses of Parliament, 1834.* Painted 1835. Joseph Mallord William Turner, English. W. 123.2 cm. 42.647

*Fluelen–Lake of Lucerne.* Water color. Joseph Mallord William Turner, English, 1775-1851. W. 47.6 cm. 54.129

*The Eve of the Deluge.* Dated 1848. Canvas. John Linnell, Sr., English. W. 223.5 cm. 72.119

*Branch Hill Pond, Hampstead Heath.* Canvas. John Constable, English, 1776-1837. W. 78 cm. 72.48

*Ville-d'Avray. A Peasant Cutting Reeds in a Swamp.* Canvas. Jean Baptiste Camille Corot, French, 1796-1875. W. 99 cm. 44.80

*Coast near Villerville.* Dated 1855. Canvas. Charles François Daubigny, French. W. 116 cm. 51.323

*Saint Etienne-du-Mont.* Etching, state I/VIII. 1852. Charles Meryon, French. H. 25.1 cm. 55.528

*Connoisseurs.* Charcoal, pencil, and water color. Honoré Victorin Daumier, French, 1808-1879. H. 26.2 cm. 27.208

*The Troubadour.* Canvas. Honoré Victorin Daumier, French, 1808-1879. H. 83.2 cm. 58.23

*Bust of a Lady.* Terra cotta. Dated 1875. Jules Dalou, French. H. 61.6 cm. 67.31

*Madame Laure Borreau (La Dame au Chapeau noir).* Dated 1863. Canvas. Gustave Courbet, French. H. 81 cm. 62.2

*Bust of a Lady.* Marble. Dated 1872. Jean-Baptiste Carpeaux, French. H. 83.2 cm. 75.5

211

*Landscape.* Black chalk. Gustave Courbet, French, 1819-1877. W. 52.6 cm. 76.18

*Grand Panorama of the Alps with the Dents du Midi.* Canvas. Ca. 1875. Gustave Courbet, French. W. 209 cm. 64.420

*Portrait of Berthe Morisot.* Oil on canvas. Ca. 1869. Edouard Manet, French. H. 73.6 cm. 58.34

*Mlle. Claire Campbell.* Pastel. 1875. Edouard Manet, French. H. 56.9 cm. 56.718

*Portrait of Madame Henry Lerolle.* Dated 1882. Canvas. Henri Fantin-Latour, French. H. 108.6 cm. 69.54

212

*Summer.* Dated 1891. Canvas. Pierre Puvis de Chavannes, French. W. 232.5 cm. 16.1056

*Blacksmiths.* Canvas. Ca. 1873/85. Charles-Emile Jacque, French. H. 116.8 cm. 73.184

*Mother and Children.* Dated 1879. Canvas. William Adolphe Bouguereau, French. H. 164.5 cm. 432.15

*Madame Henry Lerolle and Daughter Yvonne.* Painted 1879-1880. Canvas. Albert Besnard, French. H. 165.1 cm. 77.120

*The Little Milkmaid.* Canvas. Théodule Ribot, French, 1823-1891. H. 46.3 cm. 73.31

213

*Boats.* Oil on canvas. 1873.
Edouard Manet, French. W. 55.9 cm.
40.534

*Study for an Angel Blowing a Trumpet.* Black chalk.
Ca. 1857. Hilaire-Germain Edgar Degas, French.
W. 54.2 cm. 76.130

*Portrait of the Duchess of
Montejasi-Cicerale.* Oil on canvas.
1868. Hilaire-Germain Edgar Degas,
French. H. 48.9 cm. 58.28

*Portrait of Diego Martelli.* Charcoal
and white chalk on brown paper.
1879. Hilaire-Germain Edgar Degas,
French. H. 44 cm. 53.268

*Dancer.* Bronze. 1896-1897.
Hilaire-Germain Edgar Degas, French.
H. 45.7 cm. 2028.47

*Ballet Girls.* Pastel on paper, pasted on cardboard. 1897. Hilaire-Germain Edgar Degas, French. H. 55.3 cm. 16.1043

*Frieze of Dancers.* Oil on canvas. Ca. 1883. Hilaire-Germain Edgar Degas, French. W. 200.6 cm. 46.83

*Race Horses.* Pastel on cardboard. Ca. 1873-1875. Hilaire-Germain Edgar Degas, French. W. 65.4 cm. 58.27

*Esterel Village.* Monotype. Hilaire-Germain Edgar Degas, French, 1834-1917. W. 39.9 cm. 66.177

215

*Mlle. Romaine Lacaux.* Dated 1864. Oil on canvas. Pierre Auguste Renoir, French. H. 81 cm. 42.1065

*The Artist's Sister, Mme. Pontillon, Seated on the Grass.* Oil on canvas. 1873. Berthe Morisot, French. W. 72.4 cm. 50.89

*Le Fond de l'Hermitage.* Dated 1879. Oil on canvas. Camille Pissarro, French. W. 163.2 cm. 51.356

*The Cowherdess, Eragny.* Charcoal. Camille Pissarro, French, 1830-1903. H. 39.3 cm. 2609.47

216

*Spring Flowers.* Dated 1864. Oil on canvas.
Claude Oscar Monet, French. H. 116.9 cm. 53.155

*La Capeline Rouge—Madame Monet.* Oil on canvas.
Ca. 1870. Claude Oscar Monet, French. H. 100.3 cm.
58.39

*Low Tide at Pourville near Dieppe.* Dated 1882.
Oil on canvas. Claude Oscar Monet, French. W. 81.3 cm.
47.196

*Antibes.* Oil on canvas. 1888. Claude Oscar Monet,
French. W. 91.4 cm. 16.1044

217

*Saint-Mammès, Loing Canal.* Dated 1885. Oil on canvas. Alfred Sisley, French. W. 53.3 cm. 61.262

*Portrait of a Woman (Meditation?).* Oil on canvas. Ca. 1891. Edmond François Aman-Jean, French. W. 89.9 cm. 72.120

*The Age of Bronze.* Bronze. 1876. Auguste Rodin, French. H. 180.8 cm. 18.328

*William E. Henley.* Bronze. 1882. Auguste Rodin, French. H. 41.6 cm. 40.581

*The Jewish Boy.* Wax. 1892-1893. Medardo Rosso, Italian. H. 22.3 cm. 70.33

*The Judgment of Paris.* Bronze. 1914. Pierre Auguste
Renoir (and Richard Guino), French. H. 74.3 cm. 41.591

*Madame C.* Oil on canvas. Ca. 1880. Eugène
Carrière, French. W. 46 cm. 67.126

*Three Bathers.* Oil on canvas. 1897.
Pierre Auguste Renoir, French. W. 65.7 cm. 39.269

*The Apple Seller.* Oil on canvas. Ca. 1890.
Pierre Auguste Renoir, French. H. 65.7 cm. 58.47

*Young Woman Arranging Her Earrings.*
Oil on canvas. 1905.
Pierre Auguste Renoir, French.
H. 55.3 cm.  51.324

*Siesta.* Red chalk. Pierre Auguste
Renoir, French, 1841-1919.
H. 30.9 cm.  49.551

*The Pigeon Tower at Bellevue.* Oil on canvas. Ca. 1894-1896.
Paul Cézanne, French. W. 80 cm.  36.19

*The Brook.* Oil on canvas. Ca. 1898-1900. Paul Cézanne, French.
H. 80.7 cm.  58.20

*La Montagne Sainte-Victoire.* Oil on canvas.
Ca. 1894-1900. Paul Cézanne, French. W. 92.1 cm.
58.21

*The Bathers* (small plate). Lithograph printed in colors.
Paul Cézanne, French, 1839-1906. W. 29 cm. 63.598

*Water Lilies.* Oil on canvas. Ca. 1919-1922. Claude Oscar Monet, French.
W. 425.5 cm. 60.81

*Mademoiselle Ravoux.* Oil on canvas. 1890.
Vincent van Gogh, Dutch (French School). Sq. 50.2 cm.
58.31

*Poplars on a Hill.* Oil on canvas. 1889.
Vincent van Gogh, Dutch (French School). H. 61 cm.
58.32

*The Road Menders at Arles.* Oil on canvas. 1889.
Vincent van Gogh, Dutch (French School). W. 92.1 cm.
47.209

*Rodin Working the Gates of Hell.*
Bronze. 1910. Emile Antoine
Bourdelle, French. H. 68.3 cm.
43.291

222

*May Belfort.* Oil on cardboard.
1895. Henri de Toulouse-Lautrec,
French. H. 62.9 cm.  58.54

*The Laundress.* Brush and black
ink, heightened with white
on scratchboard. 1888.
Henri de Toulouse-Lautrec, French.
H. 76.2 cm.  52.113

*Monsieur Boileau at the Café.* Gouache on cardboard.
1893. Henri de Toulouse-Lautrec, French. H. 80 cm.
394.25

*The Jockey.* Dated 1899. Lithograph.
Henri de Toulouse-Lautrec, French.
H. 51.8 cm.  67.234

*Banks of the Seine at Suresnes.* Oil on panel. 1883.
Georges Seurat, French. W. 26.5 cm. 58.51

*Café Concert.* Conte crayon with
touches of white. Georges Seurat,
French, 1859-1891. H. 30.8 cm.
58.344

*L'appel (The Call).* Dated 1902. Oil on canvas.
Paul Gauguin, French. H. 130.2 cm. 43.392

*Head of a Tahitian Woman.* Pencil.
Paul Gauguin, French, 1848-1903.
H. 30.6 cm. 49.439

*Vase of Flowers.* Oil on canvas. Ca. 1905.
Odilon Redon, French. H. 73 cm. 35.233

*Orpheus.* Pastel. Painted after 1913.
Odilon Redon, French. H. 69.8 cm. 26.25

*Portrait of Mademoiselle Violette Heymann.* Dated 1910.
Pastel. Odilon Redon, French. W. 92.5 cm. 1976.26

*Closed Eyes.* Lithograph. Odilon
Redon, French, 1840-1916.
H. 31.7 cm. 27.306

225

*The Slopes of the Bay, Beg-ar-Fry.* Dated 1895.
Oil on canvas. Maxime Maufra, French. W. 60 cm.
66.382

*The Café Wepler.* Oil on canvas. Ca. 1905.
Edouard Vuillard, French. W. 103.2 cm. 50.90

*La Porte de Saint-Cloud.* Dated 1904. Oil on canvas.
Pierre Albert Marquet, French. W. 81.3 cm. 61.263

*Under the Trees.* Dated 1894.
Tempera on canvas. Edouard Vuillard,
French. H. 214.6 cm. 53.212

*La Terrasse de Café.* Oil on cardboard. 1898.
Pierre Bonnard, French. W. 48 cm. 76.148

*The Dessert.* Oil on canvas. 1921. Pierre Bonnard,
French. W. 80 cm. 49.18

*Cabinet.* Wood marquetry with metal mounts. Ca. 1910.
Louis Majorelle, French. Approx. W. 162.6 cm.
76.53

227

*Easter Egg.* Lapis lazuli, gold, pearls, rubies, diamonds, enamel. Late 19th-early 20th century. Firm of Carl Fabergé, Russian, St. Petersburg. H. 5.9 cm. 66.436

*Miniature Bidet.* Gold, jade, enamel, and pearls. Made after 1903. Firm of Carl Fabergé; Henrik Wigström, workmaster, Russian, St. Petersburg. H. 8.3 cm. 66.455

*View of Florence from San Miniato.* Canvas. 1837.
Thomas Cole, American. W. 160.3 cm.  61.39

*Schroon Mountain, The Adirondacks.* Dated 1838. Canvas.
Thomas Cole, American. W. 160 cm.  1335.17

*View Near Newport.* Canvas. Ca. 1860.
John Frederick Kensett, American.
W. 55.9 cm.  46.255

*October Day in the White Mountains.* Dated 1854.
Canvas. John Frederick Kensett, American. W. 122.9 cm.
67.5

229

*Twilight in the Wilderness.* Dated
1860. Canvas. Frederic Edwin
Church, American. W. 162.6 cm.
65.233

*Portrait of Geneo Scott.* Dated 1859. Canvas. Eastman
Johnson, American. W. 127 cm. 54.475

*Point Judith, Rhode Island.* Canvas. Ca. 1867/8.
Martin Johnson Heade, American. W. 128 cm. 70.161

*A Home in the Wilderness.* Dated 1866. Canvas. Sanford
Robinson Gifford, American. W. 77.5 cm. 70.162

*The Venetian Girl.* Canvas. Frank
Duveneck, American, 1848-1919.
H. 86.4 cm. 22.173

*The Balcony.* Etching, state I/XI.
James McNeill Whistler, American,
1834-1903. H. 29.5 cm. 40.1088

*The Devil and Tom Walker.* Dated 1856. Canvas.
John Quidor, American. W. 87.3 cm. 67.18

*Approaching Storm from the Alban Hills.* Dated 187[?].
Canvas. George Inness, American. W. 113 cm. 27.396

*The Boat Builder.* Canvas. John George
Brown, American, 1831-1913. W. 101.6 cm.
905.72

*The Briarwood Pipe.* Dated 1864. Canvas.
Winslow Homer, American. H. 42.9 cm. 44.524

*The Clambake.* Dated 1873. Water color. Winslow
Homer, American. W. 35.3 cm. 45.229

*Boy with the Anchor.* Dated 1873. Water color.
Winslow Homer, American. W. 34.9 cm. 54.128

*Early Morning After a Storm at Sea.* Canvas. 1902.
Winslow Homer, American. W. 127 cm. 24.195

*Biglin Brothers Turning the Stake.* Dated 1873.
Canvas. Thomas Eakins, American. W. 153 cm. 1984.27

*Capri.* Dated 1869. Canvas. William Stanley
Haseltine, American. W. 80.2 cm. 75.4

233

*Rishi Calling up a Storm.* Water color. John
La Farge, American, 1835-1910. W. 32.7 cm.  39.267

*Portrait of Miss Dora Wheeler.* Canvas. 1883. William
Merritt Chase, American. W. 165.8  21.1239

*The Race Track,* or *Death on a Pale Horse.* Canvas.
Ca. 1910. Albert Pinkham Ryder, American. W. 89.5 cm.
28.8

*After the Bath.* Pastel. Ca. 1901. Mary Cassatt, American (French School). W. 99.7 cm. 20.379

*Building a Dam, Shetucket.* Canvas. 1908. J. Alden Weir, American. W. 102.2 cm. 27.171

*The Visitor.* Drawing. Mary Cassatt, American (French School), 1845-1926. H. 40 cm. 66.176

*Fifth Avenue Nocturne.* Canvas. Ca. 1895. Childe Hassam, American. H. 61.2 cm. 52.538

*Vase.* Glass. 1915. Louis Comfort Tiffany, American. H. 19.9 cm. 70.126

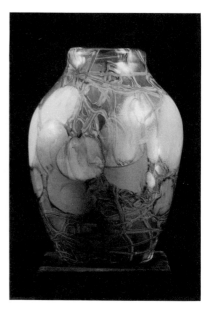

*The Drive, Central Park.* Canvas. Ca. 1905.
William J. Glackens, American. W. 81.3 cm. 39.524

*Self-Portrait.* Dated 191(8?). Panel. Abbott
Handerson Thayer, American. H. 88.9 cm. 70.17

*Window.* Glass. Ca. 1900-1901.
Louis Comfort Tiffany, American.
H. 227.2 cm. 66.432

*May Day, Central Park.* Dated 1901. Water color.
Maurice Prendergast, American, W. 50.2 cm. 26.17

236

*Card Rack with Jack of Hearts.* Painted after 1894.
Canvas. John Frederick Peto, American. H. 76.2 cm.
73.30

*Self-Portrait (George Bellows Drawing
on a Stone in His Study).* Lithograph.
1921. George Wesley Bellows,
American. H. 26.7 cm. 35.279

*Stag at Sharkey's.* Canvas. 1907. George Wesley Bellows,
American. W. 122.5 cm. 1133.22

*Holiday on the Hudson.* Canvas. Ca. 1912.
George Benjamin Luks, American. W. 91.7 cm.
2291.33

*Still Life.* Oil on canvas. Preston Dickinson,
American, 1891-1930. W. 76.5 cm. 1664.26

*Church Bells Ringing, Rainy Winter Night.* Dated 1917.
Water color on paper. Charles E. Burchfield, American.
H. 76.2 cm. 49.544

*The Sunflower Arch.* Dated 1917.
Indelible pencil and crayon.
Charles E. Burchfield, American.
H. 50.5 cm. 65.461

*Fireworks.* Dated 1926. Water color. George Overbury ("Pop") Hart, American. W. 70.5 cm. 38.125

*Woman's Work.* Canvas. John Sloan, American, 1871-1951. H. 80.3 cm. 64.160

*Hills, South Truro.* Canvas. 1930. Edward Hopper, American. W. 109.5 cm. 2647.31

*Rock and Sea, Small Point, Maine.* Dated 1931. Canvas. John Marin, American. W. 71 cm. 56.361

239

*Landscape, New Mexico.* Canvas. Marsden Hartley, American, 1878-1943. W. 90.8 cm. 30.665

*Storm-Frightened Animals.* Oil on canvas. 1933. Henry G. Keller, American. W. 101.6 cm. 34.56

*Hills, South Truro.* Canvas. 1930. Edward Hopper, American. W. 109.5 cm. 2647.31

*Horses in Snow.* Water color. Ca. 1933. William Sommer, American. W. 54.6 cm. 33.24

*Wounded Scoter, No. 2.* Water color on rice paper
mounted on cloth. 1944. Morris Graves, American.
W. 75.9 cm.  45.231

*The Vengeance of Hop-Frog.* Etching,
state II/II. James Ensor, Belgian,
1860-1949. H. 35.9 cm.  70.38

*Deserted Farm.* Canvas. 1943. Max Weber, American.
W. 123.2 cm.  210.46

*Seated Female Nude.* Charcoal.
Paula Modersohn-Becker, German,
1876-1907. H. 62.2 cm.  73.35

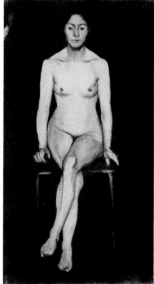

*Woman with Cape.* Oil on canvas.
Ca. 1901. Pablo Picasso, Spanish
(French School). H. 73 cm. 58.44

*The Donkey Driver.* Dated 1902.
Pencil. Pablo Picasso, Spanish
(French School). H. 26.1 cm.
58.12

*Two Nude Women.* Lithograph, state
VIII/XVIII. Pablo Picasso, Spanish
(French School), 1881-1973.
W. 43 cm. 72.57

*La Vie.* Oil on canvas. 1903.
Pablo Picasso, Spanish (French
School). H. 196.5 cm. 45.24

*Head of a Boy.* Dated 1905. Gouache
on composition board fastened to
panel. Pablo Picasso, Spanish (French
School). H. 31 cm. 58.43

*Figures in Pink.* Oil on canvas.
1905. Pablo Picasso, Spanish
(French School). H. 154.3 cm. 58.45

242

*Fan, Salt Box, Melon.* Oil on canvas. 1909.
Pablo Picasso, Spanish (French School). H. 81.3 cm.
69.22

*Bottle, Glass, and Fork.* Oil on canvas. 1912.
Pablo Picasso, Spanish (French School). H. 71.8 cm.
72.8

*Harlequin with Violin (Si Tu Veux).* Oil on canvas.
1918. Pablo Picasso, Spanish (French School).
H. 142.2 cm. 75.2

*Still Life with Violin.* Collage with gouache and
charcoal on chipboard. Ca. 1913. Georges Braque,
French. H. 71.8 cm. 68.196

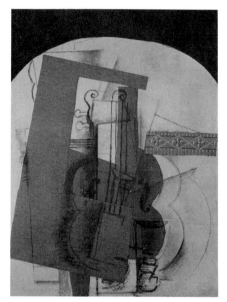

*The Crystal Vase.* Oil on canvas. 1929. Georges Braque, French.
W. 120.6 cm. 75.82

*Guitar and Bottle of Marc on a Table.*
Oil and sand on canvas. 1930.
Georges Braque, French. H. 129 cm.
75.59

*Amorpha, Fugue for Two Colors II.*
Oil on canvas. 1909-1912.
Frantisek (Frank) Kupka,
Czechoslovakian (French School).
H. 111.7 cm. 69.51

*Detachable Figure (Dancer).* Ebony
and oak. 1915. Jacques Lipchitz,
American (born in Lithuania).
H. 98.1 cm. 72.367

244

*Markwippach III.* Dated 1916. Charcoal. Lyonel
Feininger, American. W. 31.5 cm. 63.73

*Houses in Old Paris.* Woodcut. 1919.
Lyonel Feininger, American.
H. 31.3 cm. 52.27

*Markwippach.* Dated 1917. Oil on canvas.
Lyonel Feininger, American (German School). W. 101 cm.
60.180

*The Motor Boat.* Dated 1931. Oil on canvas.
Lyonel Feininger, American (German School). W. 77.5 cm.
64.53

245

*Self-Portrait with Hat.* Oil on
canvas. 1919.
Karl Schmidt-Rottluff, German.
H. 73.3 cm. 65.440

*Melancholia: On the Beach.* Hand-colored woodcut. 1896.
Edvard Munch, Norwegian. W. 45 cm. 59.82

*Wrestlers in a Circus.* Oil on canvas. Ca. 1909.
Ernst Ludwig Kirchner, German. W. 94 cm. 66.49

*Mountain Landscape with Fir Trees.* Pencil and brush and
India ink. Ernst Ludwig Kirchner, German, 1880-1938.
W. 50.6 cm. 63.86

246

*Karneval im Schnee (Carnival in the Snow).* Water color. 1923. Paul Klee, Swiss (German School). H. 26.6 cm. 69.46

*Forest.* Painted wood. 1916 (1917 ?). Jean (Hans) Arp, French (Alsatian). W. 50.8 cm. 70.52

*Madonna and Child.* Pen and ink wash. 1943. Henry Spencer Moore, English. H. 22.5 cm. 313.47

*Male Torso.* Dated 1917. Brass. Constantin Brancusi, Roumanian (French School). H. 46.7 cm. 3205.37

*Mother and Child.* Bronze. 1929-1930. Jacques Lipchitz, American (born in Lithuania). H. 130.2 cm. 55.166

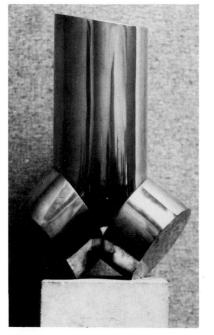

*Autumn Landscape.* Dated 1926. Lithograph printed in colors. Emil Nolde, German. W. 80.8 cm. 70.353

*Woman and Bird.* Dated 1944. Oil on canvas. Rufino Tamayo, Mexican. H. 106.7 cm. 50.583

*The Wounded Soldier.* Oil on canvas. 1930. José Clemente Orozco, Mexican. H. 113 cm. 54.864

*Head of Christ.* Oil on canvas. 1938. Georges Rouault, French. H. 104.8 cm. 50.399

*Carnival at Nice.* Oil on canvas. Ca. 1923.
Henri Matisse, French. W. 95.2 cm. 46.444

*Interior with Etruscan Vase.* Dated 1940. Oil on
canvas. Henri Matisse, French. W. 108 cm. 52.153

*Potager à la Brunié (Kitchen Garden at Brunie).*
Dated 1941. Oil on canvas. Jacques Villon, French.
W. 92 cm. 64.95

*Constellation: Woman with Blond Armpit Combing Her
Hair by the Light of the Stars.* Oil and gouache on
paper. 1940. Joan Miró, Spanish. W. 46 cm. 65.2

249

*Through the Windshield (La Route a Villacoublay).*
Oil on canvas. 1917. Henri Matisse, French.
W. 55.9 cm. 72.225

*Untitled (Landscape?).* Oil and pencil on canvas. 1943.
Arshile Gorky, American. W. 63.5 cm. 63.152

*The Chrysanthemum.* Dated 1906.
Oil on canvas. Piet Mondrian,
Dutch. H. 41.6 cm. 58.38

*Composition with Red, Yellow, and Blue.* Dated 1927.
Oil on canvas. Piet Mondrian, Dutch. Sq. 51.1 cm.
67.215

*Mallarmé's Swan.* Dated 1944.
Collage with gouache, crayon, and
paper on cardboard.
Robert Motherwell, American.
H. 110.5 cm. 61.229

*Figure.* Oil on cardboard. 1949.
Willem de Kooning, American (born
in Holland). H. 46.7 cm. 64.1

*Smaragd Red and Germinating
Yellow.* Dated 1959. Oil on canvas.
Hans Hofmann, American (born in
Germany). H. 139.7 cm. 60.57

*Elegy to the Spanish Republic No. LV.* Oil on canvas.
1955-1960. Robert Motherwell, American. W. 193.3 cm.
63.583

*Red Maroons.* Dated 1962. Oil on canvas. Mark Rothko,
American (born in Russia). W. 205.7 cm. 62.239

*Mandrake.* Steel brazed with copper. 1951.
Theodore Roszak, American (born in Poland). W. 101.6 cm.
64.4

*Untitled, No. 2.* Dated 1961. Pastel on paper mounted
on cardboard. Adja Yunkers, American (born in Latvia).
W. 175.3 cm. 66.138

*Untitled.* Painted metal. 1959.
John Angus Chamberlain, American.
H. 82.5 cm. 73.27

*All Whites.* Embroidery, mixed wool,
linen, cotton, and asbestos yarns on
mohair. Ca. 1954. Mariska Karasz,
American (born in Hungary).
H. 171 cm. 54.287

*Composition Circulaire.* Tempera on
panel. 1960. Mark Tobey,
American. D. 17.8 cm. 63.150

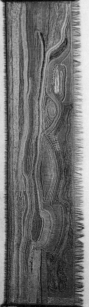

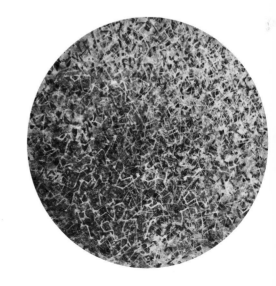

252

*Accent Grave.* Oil on canvas. 1955. Franz Kline,
American. H. 191.1 cm.  67.3

*Berkeley.* Dated 1955. Oil on canvas.
Richard Diebenkorn, American. H. 146 cm.  68.95

*Video.* Construction of mixed media. Joseph Cornell,
American, 1903-1972. W. 36.8 cm.  64.143

253

*Composition Concrete* (Study for Mural). Oil on canvas. 1957-1960. Stuart Davis, American. H. 108.7 cm. 64.2

*Crest.* Oil on canvas. 1958. Jack Tworkov, American (born in Poland). H. 190.5 cm. 62.33

*Sleeper I.* Oil on canvas. 1958. Philip Guston, American (born in Canada). W. 193 cm. 61.21

*Pilgrim.* Steel. 1957. David Smith, American. H. 207 cm. 66.385

*First Theme.* Oil on canvas. 1963. Burgoyne Diller, American. H. 228.6 cm. 73.211

*Woman with Child.* White marble. 1958. Isamu Noguchi, American. H. 111.3 cm. 66.48

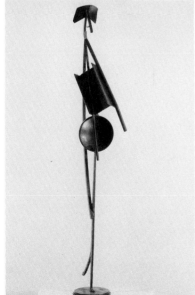

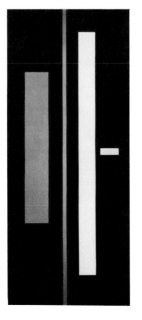

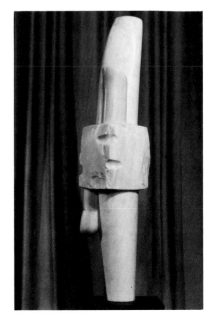

*Untitled.* Acrylic on canvas. 1969.
Larry Poons, American. H. 342.9 cm.
69.49

*Fragmented Figure Construction.*
Welded steel. 1963. Richard Hunt,
American. H. 143.5 cm. 69.16

*Sky Cathedral—Moon Garden Wall.* Wood, painted black.
1956-1959. Louise Nelson, American (born in Russia).
H. 217.5 cm. 74.76

*Red Blue.* Oil on canvas. 1962. Ellsworth Kelly,
American. H. 228.6 cm. 64.142

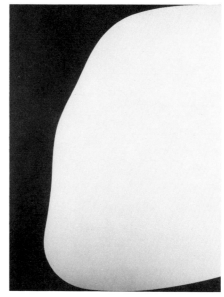

*Reconstruction.* Dated 1959. Encaustic and canvas collage on canvas. Jasper Johns, American. H. 155 cm. 73.28

*Louis II.* Dated 1962. Oil on canvas. Richard Lindner, American (born in Germany). H. 127 cm. 65.450

*Gloria.* Oil and paper collage on canvas. 1956. Robert Rauschenberg, American. H. 168.3 cm. 66.333

*Nyack.* Dated 1966-1967. Oil on canvas. Fairfield Porter, American. W. 279.4 cm. 68.3

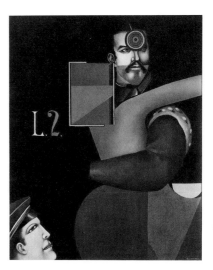

*Number 99.* Acrylic on canvas. 1959. Morris Louis, American. W. 360.6 cm. 68.110

*Grey Morning.* Stitching, cutwork, and appliqué on wool. 1967. Evelyn Svec Ward, American. W. 94 cm. 67.201

*Wending Back.* Painted steel. 1969-1970. Anthony Caro, English. W. 320 cm. 70.29

*The Red Light.* Plaster and mixed media. 1972. George Segal, American. H. 289.5 cm. 74.22

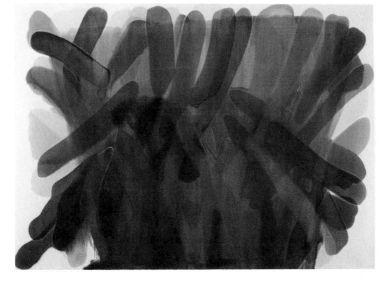

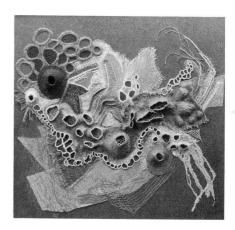

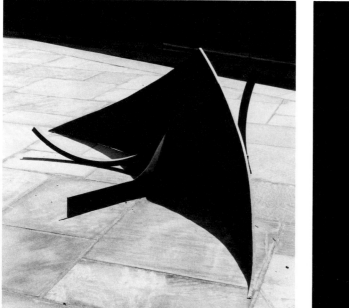

*Grey Pilgrim.* Acrylic on canvas.
1971. Kenneth Noland, American.
H. 240 cm.  72.250

*New Shoes for H.* Acrylic on canvas. 1973-1974.
Don Eddy, American. W. 121.9 cm.  74.53

*Omsk Measure II.* Acrylic on canvas. 1972.
Jules Olitski, American (born in Russia). H. 276.3 cm.
73.25

*Knight Series OC #1.* Oil on canvas. 1975.
Jack Tworkov, American (born in Poland). H. 228.5 cm.
76.102

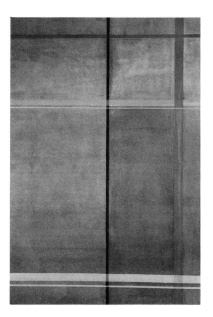

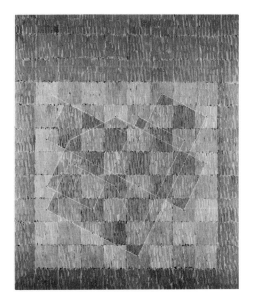

258

*Georgia O'Keeffe.* Photograph,
silver print. 1933. Alfred Stieglitz,
American. H. 24 cm.  35.52

*Colette.* Dated 1951. Photograph, silver print.
Irving Penn, American. H. 55.9 cm.  66.141

*The Black Sun, Tugsten Hills, Owens Valley, California.*
Photograph, silver print. 1939. Ansel Adams,
American. W. 46.8 cm.  73.119

*Henri Matisse.* Photograph, silver print. 1944.
Henri Cartier-Bresson, French. W. 35.7 cm.  73.123

*Bijou.* Photograph, silver print. 1932. Brassaï (Gyula Halász), French (born in Hungary). H. 30.9 cm. 73.121

*Beginnings, Frosted Window* (Rochester, New York). Photograph, silver print. 1962. Minor White, American. H. 29.5 cm. 74.225

*Marie Spartali.* Photograph, albumen print. Ca. 1872. Julia Margaret Cameron, English. W. 35.7 cm. 74.52

*Alabama Cotton Tenant Farmer's Wife.* Photograph, silver print. 1936. Walker Evans, American. H. 23.6 cm. 73.120

*Untitled* (Smokestacks). Photograph, silver print. Ca. 1927-1929. Margaret Bourke-White, American. H. 33.4 cm. 74.215

*Funeral Cortege.* Dated 1938. Photograph, silver print. Dorothea Lange, American. H. 28 cm. 65.328

# Notes

# Islamic Art

264

*Gold Ewer.* Repoussé and engraved.
Iran, Buyid Period, reign of
Samsam al-Dawla, 985-998.
H. 12.1 cm.  66.22

*Tombstone.* Marble. Iran, Seljuk
Period, 1110. H. 64.5 cm.  50.9

*Hitching Post.* Limestone. Iran,
Seljuk Period, 13th century.
H. 62.9 cm.  44.481

*End of Balustrade.* Limestone. Iran,
Hamadan, Mongol Period, 1304.
H. 66.7 cm.  38.15

*Lion Incense Burner.* Bronze, cast
and engraved. Iran, Seljuk Period,
12th century. H. 36 cm.  48.308

265

*Bird-Shaped Vessel.* Bronze, cast and engraved, with turquoise eyes. Iran, Seljuk Period, 12th-13th century. H. 17.5 cm. 48.458

*Footed Bowl.* Bronze, inlaid with silver. Iran, Seljuk Period, early 13th century. H. 11.5 cm. 44.485

*Ewer.* Dated 1223. Brass, inlaid with silver. Made by Ahmad al-Dhaki, al-Naqsh, al-Mawsili, Iraq, Mosul. H. 38.1 cm. 56.11

*Tray.* Brass, inlaid with silver. Syria, mid-13th century. D. 54 cm. 45.386

*Candlestick.* Brass, inlaid with silver and engraved. Syria, 13th century. H. 24.8 cm. 51.539

266

*Box.* Bronze, inlaid with gold and
silver. Syria, 13th century.
H. 9.9 cm. 44.482

*Pottery Bowl.* Luster ware. Egypt,
Fustat, 11th century. D. 25.4 cm.
44.476

*Bottle.* Enameled glass. Egypt or
Syria, Mamluke Period, 14th century.
H. 44.1 cm. 44.488

*Bowl.* Enameled glass. Egypt or Syria, Mamluke Period,
14th century. D. 31.8 cm. 44.235

*Pottery Bowl.* Polychrome painted
ware. Iran, Nishapur, 10th century.
D. 28 cm. 56.225

*Pottery Bowl.* Polychrome painted ware. Iran, Nishapur, 10th century. D. 35.6 cm. 59.249

*Pottery Bowl.* Champlevé ware. Iran, Garruz district, 11th-12th century. D. 39.2 cm. 38.8

*Pottery Bowl.* Lakabi ware. Iran, 11th-12th century. D. 40.7 cm. 38.7

*Pottery Jug.* Underglaze slip-painted ware. Iran, 12th century. H. 13.4 cm. 47.495

*Pottery Plate.* Luster ware. Iran, Gurgan, 12th-13th century. D. 39.4 cm. 51.289

268

*Pottery Bottle.* Luster ware. Iran, Rayy, 12th-13th century. H. 35.5 cm. 15.525

*Pottery Wall Tile.* Luster ware. Iran, Kashan, 1266. H. 20.3 cm. 15.524

*Pottery Beaker.* Minai ware. Iran, Rayy, early 13th century. H. 13.8 cm. 17.977

*Pottery Bowl.* Minai ware. Iran, Rayy, early 13th century. D. 21.7 cm. 39.214

*Mihrab and Frieze.* Faience mosaic tiles. Iran, Isfahan, 1st half 16th century. H. 290.8 cm. 62.23

269

*Tunic Ornament.* Tapestry weave, wool and linen. Egypt, Abbasid Period, 2nd half 8th century. H. 23.5 cm. 69.38

*Textile Panel.* Tapestry weave, wool and linen. Egypt, Abbasid Period, 1st half 9th century. W. 83 cm. 59.48

*Tiraz.* Tapestry weave, silk on linen. Egypt, Fatimid Period, reign of Mustanzir, 1036-1094. Over-all: H. 39.3 cm. Detail: H. 15 cm. 50.528

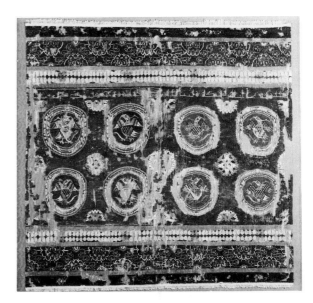

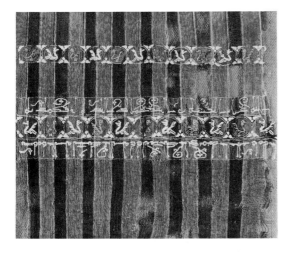

*Textile.* Tapestry weave, silk and gold on linen. Egypt, Fatimid Period, late 11th century. H. 16.5 cm. 50.541

*Textile.* Tapestry weave, silk and linen. Egypt, Fatimid Period, early 12th century. H. 13 cm. 52.255

*Textile.* Embroidery, silk and gold on *mulham.* Egypt or Sicily, 12th century. Over-all: W. 21.6 cm. Detail: H. 7.3 cm. 50.533

*Textile:* Block-printed tabby, cotton. Egypt, Fatimid Period, 12th century. H. 17.2 cm. 29.845

*Textile.* Lampas weave, silk and gold. Egypt, Mamluk Period, 14th century. Over-all: W. 111 cm. Detail: H. 70 cm. 39.40

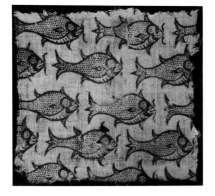

271

*Textile.* Lampas weave, silk. Iran,
Abbasid Period, 9th century.
H. 103.2 cm.  71.23

*Textile.* Lampas weave, silk. Iran,
Abbasid Period, 9th century.
H. 46 cm.  71.24

*Textile.* Lampas weave, silk. Iran,
Abbasid Period, 9th century.
H. 74.3 cm.  71.25

*Fragment of a Tomb Cover.* Compound twill, silk. Iran,
Buyid Period, AD 998. H. 78.1 cm.  55.52

*Textile.* Painted *mulham.* Iraq
(Mesopotamia), 10th century. Over-all:
W. 40 cm.  Detail: H. 26.7 cm.
50.558

*Tomb Cover.* Compound twill, silk. Iran, Buyid Period, 10th century. H. 210 cm. 54.780

*Part of a Textile Panel.* Lampas weave, silk. Iran, Buyid Period, AD 1003. H. 71 cm. 61.34

*Textile.* Lampas weave, silk. Iran, Seljuk Period, late 11th century. W. 66 cm. 75.38

*Textile Panel.* Lampas weave, silk. Iran, Buyid Period, 10th-11th century. H. 171 cm. 62.264

*Textile.* Lampas weave, silk. Iran, Buyid Period, 10th-11th century. Over-all: W. 44.5 cm. Detail: H. 30.5 cm. 50.84

273

*Textile.* Lampas weave, silk. Iran,
Buyid Period, 10th-11th century.
Over-all: H. 56.5 cm.
Detail: H. 26.2 cm. 53.434

*Textile.* Lampas weave, silk. Iran,
Buyid Period, 10th-11th century.
H. 60 cm. 68.73

*Textile.* Lampas weave, silk. Iran,
Seljuk Period, 12th century.
H. 19.5 cm. 68.223

*Textile.* Velvet weave, gold and
silk. Iran, Safavid Period,
reign of Shah Tahmasp, 1524-1576.
H. 70 cm. 48.205

*Textile.* Lampas weave, silk. Iran,
Herat, Safavid Period, early 16th
century. H. 83.5 cm. 24.743

*Fragment of a Carpet.* Senna knot, wool and cotton. Iran, Safavid Period, 16th century. Over-all: W. 185.5 cm. Detail: H. 85 cm. 53.128

*Carpet.* Single-warp knot, wool. Spain, Alcarez (?), 2nd half 15th century. Over-all: H. 480.5 cm. Detail: H. 274.5 cm. 52.511

*Carpet.* Senna knot, wool and cotton. Iran, Herat, Safavid Period, 16th century. Over-all: H. 863.5 cm. Detail: H. 752 cm. 62.263

*Carpet.* Senna knot, silk and cotton. Iran, Isfahan, Safavid Period, ca. 1600. H. 206.5 cm. 26.533

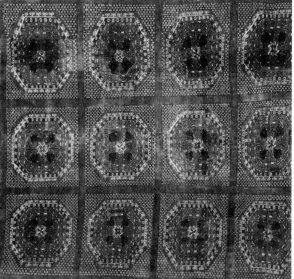

275

*Textile.* Lampas weave, silk and gold. Spain, Almeria, 12th century. H. 43.2 cm.  50.146

*Textile.* Lampas weave, silk and gold. Spain, Almeria, 12th century. H. 36.5 cm.  52.15

*Textile.* Compound twill, silk. Spain, 11th-12th century. Over-all: W. 102 cm. Detail: H. 52.4 cm.  51.92

*Textile.* Compound weave, silk and gold. Spain, Almeria, 13th century. H. 16.5 cm.  32.137

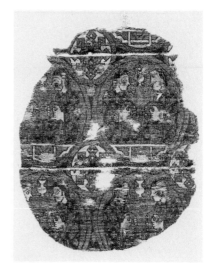

*Textile.* Velvet weave, silk. Iran, Safavid Period, 2nd half 16th century. H. 31 cm. (as mounted). 44.499, 44.500

*Textile.* Velvet weave, silk and gold. Iran, Safavid Period, 17th century. H. 155.2 cm. 32.42

*Textile.* Velvet weave, silk and gold. Iran, Safavid Period, 16th century. Over-all: H. 77.5 cm. Detail: H. 53.2 cm. 44.239

*Textile.* Lampas weave, silk and gold. Iran, Safavid Period, 17th century. Over-all: H. 87.5 cm. Detail: H. 56 cm. 53.17

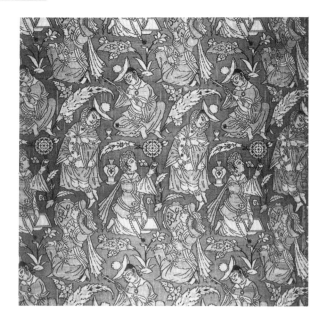

277

*Textile.* Tapestry weave, silk and
gold. Spain, Hispano-Islamic
Period, 13th century. H. 17.5 cm.
52.105

*Textile.* Lampas weave, silk and
gold. Spain, Almeria, 13th century.
H. 9.9 cm. 42.1077

*Textile.* Tapestry weave, silk and
gold. Hispano-Islamic Period, 13th
century. Over-all: H. 26 cm.
Detail: H. 6 cm. 28.650

*Textile.* Lampas weave, silk. Spain,
Granada, 14th century. H. 76.8 cm.
46.417

*Textile.* Lampas weave, silk and
gold. Spain, Granada, 14th
century. H. 47.6 cm. 39.35

*Textile.* Lampas weave, silk. Spain,
Granada, 14th century. Over-all:
H. 50.8 cm. Detail: H. 40 cm. 40.609

278

*Illustration from a Manuscript of
the Automata by Al-Jazari: Device
for Washing Hands.* Miniature
painting. Iraq, 1315. H. 31.5 cm.
45.383

*Three Physicians Preparing Medicines.*
Page from the Arabic translation of
Dioscorides' *Materia Medica.* Dated
1224. Color on paper. Abdallah ibn
al-Fadl, Iraqi, 13th century.
H. 33 cm. 77.91

*Illustration from a Manuscript of
the Shahnamah of Firdawsi:
Nushirwan's Fifth Banquet for
Buzurdjmir.* Miniature painting.
Iran, Tabriz, Il-Khanid Period,
ca. 1330-1340. H. 24.2 cm. 59.330

*Illustration from a Manuscript of the Shahnamah of
Firdawsi: Bahram Gur Slays a Dragon.* Miniature painting.
Iran, Tabriz School (?), Il-Khanid Period, ca. 1330-
1340. H. 19.7 cm. 43.658

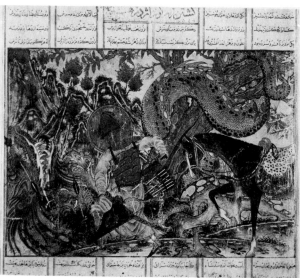

279

*Double-Page Frontispiece from a Manuscript of the Shahnamah of Firdawsi: Courtly Scene.* Miniature painting. Iran, Shiraz, Timurid Period, ca. 1440. H. 26.7 cm. 45.169, 56.10

*Illustration from a Manuscript of the Shahnamah of Firdawsi: Rustam Meets the Challenge of Ashkabus.* Miniature painting. Turkey, Provincial School, ca. 1590-1600. H. 32.5 cm. 60.199

*Garden Scene.* Miniature painting (unfinished). Iran, Herat, Timurid Period, style of Bihzad, late 15th century. H. 26.4 cm. 44.490

*A Picnic in the Mountains.* Line drawing with color. Iran, Tabriz, Safavid Period, style of Muhammadi, ca. 1550. H. 26.5 cm. 44.491

280

*Ruler Seated in a Garden.* Drawing with wash. Iran, Safavid Period, 16th century. H. 21 cm. 39.508

*Illustration from the Khamsa of Nizami: An Episode from the Story of Khusraw and Shirin.* Miniature painting. Iran, Safavid Period, 16th century. H. 21.6 cm. 47.500

*Camel with Attendant.* Drawing with wash. Iran, attributed to Sultan Muhammad, Safavid Period, mid-16th century. H. 20.3 cm. 44.489

*Illustration from the Khamsa of Nizami: Nushirwan and the Owls.* Miniature painting. Iran, Safavid Period, 16th century. H. 21.6 cm. 44.487

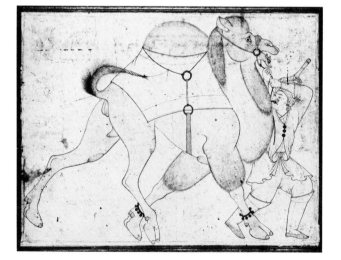

281

*Courtly Procession.* Miniature painting. Iran, Safavid
Period, ca. 1600. Detail: H. 28 cm. 62.24

*Small Black and White Bird on a Shrub Limb with
Butterflies.* Miniature painting. Shafi 'Abbasi,
Iranian, Isfahan, mid-17th century. L. 24.9 cm.
71.84

*Youth with Toy.* Miniature painting.
Iran, early 17th century. H. 26.7 cm.
47.497

*Youth Sleeping Under a Willow Tree.*
Miniature painting. Iran, Safavid
Period, late 16th century.
H. 20.8 cm. 44.494

*Bookbinding.* Leather, chased and perforated over gold. Iran, 15th century.
H. 35.9 cm. 44.495

*Dragon Combat.* Drawing. Iran, Shiraz, Turkoman, mid-16th century.
H. 17.5 cm. 44.492

# Notes

# Far Eastern Art

*Two Seals with a Bull and Unicorn.* Steatite. India, Indus Valley Period, 3000-1500 BC. H. 3.2 and 3.5 cm. 73.160, 73.161

*Fertility Ring.* Steatite. India, Maurya Period, 3rd century BC. D. 10.2 cm. 77.36

*Section of a Coping Rail.* Stone. India, Bharhut, Sunga Period, 2nd century BC. W. 122 cm. 72.366

*Center-Bead and Two Triratna-Shaped Necklace Pendants.* Gold repoussé with granulation. India, Sunga Period, 2nd-1st century BC. 73.66-73.68

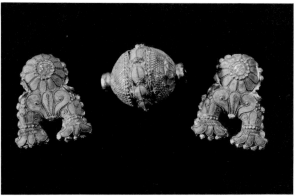

287

*Pendant with Deity Hariti.* Gold and carnelian. India, Sirkap, Saka-Parthian Period, ca. 50 BC-AD 50. D. 7.3 cm. 53.14

*Bacchanalian Scene.* Schist. India, Gandhara, from Buner, 1st-2nd century. W. 43.2 cm. 30.329

*Head of a Yaksha.* Red mottled sandstone. India, Mathura, Sunga Period, 1st century BC. H. 48.2 cm. 62.45

*Miracle at Sravasti.* Gray schist. India, Gandhara, 2nd century. W. 29.2 cm. 75.102

*Seated Buddha.* Gray schist. India, Gandhara, 3rd century. H. 129.5 cm. 61.418

*Standing Buddha.* Gray schist. India, Gandhara, 2nd-3rd century. H. 119.7 cm.  72.43

*Bodhisattva.* Gray schist. India, Gandhara, 3rd century. H. 132.4 cm. 65.476

*Adoring Attendant.* From a Buddhist shrine. Stucco. Hadda (Afghanistan), 5th century. H. 54.6 cm.  43.395

*Attendant Bearing a Fly-Whisk (Chauri).* Red sandstone. India, Mathura, Kushan Period, 2nd century. H. 55.8 cm.  65.472

*Nagaraja.* Red mottled sandstone. India, Mathura, Kushan Period, 3rd century. H. 67.3 cm.  43.661

289

*Lion.* Red mottled sandstone. India,
Mathura, Kushan Period, 2nd century.
H. 47 cm. 52.514

*Nagini.* Red mottled sandstone. India,
Mathura, Kushan Period, 2nd century.
H. 124.4 cm. 68.104

*Torana Bracket with Salabhanjikas.*
Red sandstone. India, Mathura,
Kushan Period, 2nd half 2nd
century. H. 71.1 cm. 71.15

*Railing Pillar.* Sikri sandstone.
India, Mathura, Kushan Period,
2nd-3rd century. H. 80 cm. 77.34

*Seated Buddha.* Red mottled sandstone.
India, Mathura, Kushan Period,
1st half 2nd century. H. 51.4 cm.
70.63

*Seated Buddha.* Red mottled sandstone.
India, Mathura, Kushan Period, 3rd
century. H. 64 cm. 41.94

*Seated Buddha.* Red sandstone. India, Mathura, Gupta Period, 5th century. H. 82 cm. 73.214

*Adoration of the Bodhi Tree.* Limestone. India, Amaravati, Andhra Period, 2nd century. H. 80 cm. 70.43

*Fire Pillar.* Limestone. India, Nagarjunakonda, Andhra Period, late 2nd-early 3rd century. H. 59.1 cm. 43.72

*Head of Buddha.* Red mottled sandstone. India, Mathura, Gupta Period, 5th century. H. 30.5 cm. 63.504

*Standing Buddha.* Dated AD 591. Bronze. India, Gupta Period. H. 46 cm. 68.40

291

*Standing Buddha.* Cream sandstone. India, Sarnath, Gupta Period, 5th century. H. 76.2 cm. 43.278

*Plate with Figures.* Silver alloy. India, Gupta Period, 320-600. D. 18.8 cm. 72.71

*Head of Vishnu from Besnagar.* Gray sandstone. India, Vidisha District, Madhya Pradesh, Gupta Period, 4th century. H. 40.6 cm. 69.57

*Vishnu.* Red sandstone. India, Mathura, late Gupta Period, end of 6th century. H. 109.2 cm. 63.580

*Vishnu.* Buff-colored sandstone. India, Allahabad region (?), Gupta Period, late 5th century. H. 85.4 cm. 76.75

*Head of Vishnu.* Red mottled sandstone. India, Mathura, Gupta Period, 5th century. H. 28 cm. 42.498

*Matrika from Tanesara.* Grayish-green schist. India, Rajasthan, Gupta Period, early 6th century. H. 73.4 cm. 70.12

*Yumna, Goddess of the Yumna River.* Buff red-veined sandstone. India, Mathura region, early Medieval Period, early 7th century. H. 108 cm. 66.119

*Seated Ascetics.* Two terra-cotta plaques. Kashmir, Harwan, 4th century. H. 50.8 cm. 59.131, 59.132

293

*Female Attendants Bearing Fly-Whisks (Chauri).* Ivory. Kashmir, 7th-8th century. H. 7.6 cm. 72.35, 72.36

*Temptation of Buddha by the Evil Forces of Mara.* Ivory. Kashmir, 8th century. H. 13.5 cm. 71.18

*Vajrapani: Seated Thunderbolt-Bearer.* Bronze. Kashmir, 8th century. H. 22.2 cm. 71.14

*Eleven-Headed Avalokiteśvara.* Bronze. Kashmir, 9th century. H. 39.4 cm. 75.101

*Surya, the Sun God.* Brass. Kashmir, early 8th century. H. 50.3 cm. 65.557

294

*Standing Buddha.* Brass. Kashmir, ca. 10th century. H. 98.1 cm. 66.30

*Vishnu Riding on Garuda.* Black chlorite. East India, early Pala Period, 7th century. H. 81.3 cm. 61.46

*Mukhalinga.* Black chlorite. East India, early Pala Period, 7th century. H. 83.8 cm. 73.73

*Chakrapurusa: Angel of the Discus.* Black chlorite. India, Apshad, Pala Period, ca. 670. H. 76.8 cm. 45.367

*Buddha Calling on the Earth to Witness.* Black chlorite. East India, Pala Period, 9th century. H. 94 cm. 35.146

*Akshobhya: The Buddha of the East.*
Bronze. India, Kurkihar, Bihar,
Pala Period, 9th century. H. 39.3 cm.
70.10

*Śiva and Parvati: Umamaheśvara.*
Bronze. East India, Pala Period,
reign of Devapala, 815-854.
H. 17.8 cm. 64.50

*Bodhisattva Manjuśri: Lord of
Wisdom.* Image of gilded copper;
pedestal and mandorla of brass.
East India, Pala Period, 11th-
12th century. H. 31.2 cm. 60.285

*Vishnu Attended by Chakrapurusa and
Shankhapurusa.* Bronze with silver
inlay. East India, Pala Period,
ca. 12th century. H. 43.5 cm. 64.453

*Avalokiteśvara Padmapani:
Bodhisattva of Mercy Bearing a
Lotus.* Bronze. Nepal, ca. 11th
century. H. 61.9 cm. 76.3

296

Gandavyuha: Structure of the World (detail). Illuminated
manuscript, ink and color on palm leaf. East India,
Pala Period, 11th-12th century. W. 52.4 cm. 55.49

Astasahasrika Prajnaparamita: Book of Transcendental
Wisdom (detail). Illuminated manuscript, color on wood
and palm leaf. Nepal, 1100. W. 56.2 cm. 38.301

Padmapani: Lotus-Bearing Bodhisattva.
Bronze inlaid with silver. West
Tibet, 10th-11th century. H. 26.7 cm.
76.70

Vasudhara: Goddess of Abundance.
Copper gilt with inlaid gems.
Nepal, 14th-15th century.
H. 16.3 cm. 47.493

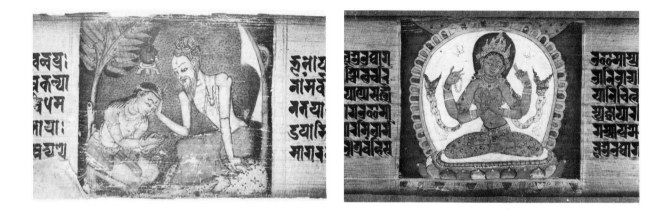

297

*Tanka with Green Tara.* Color on cloth. Nepal, 14th century. H. 52.1 cm. 70.156

*Pata with Four Figures.* Color on cloth. Tibet, 15th century. H. 57.8 cm. 60.209

*Tanka with Bejeweled Buddha Preaching.* Dated 1648. Color on cloth. Nepal. H. 110 cm. 73.69

*Manjuśri: Bodhisattva of Wisdom.* Gilt bronze. Nepal, 15th century. H. 78.1 cm. 64.370

*Manjuśri: Bodhisattva of Wisdom.* Gilt copper. Nepal, 15th century. H. 42.9 cm. 56.8

*Vajravarahi: Dancing Tantric Deity.*
Dry lacquer. Nepal, 16th-17th
century. H. 63.5 cm.  64.103

*Vaishnava Trinity: Śri Devi, Vishnu, Bhu Devi.* Granite.
India, probably from region of Pudokkatai, early Chola
Period, 1st half 10th century. H. *(Vishnu)* 175.9 cm.
63.104-63.106

*Gajasura-Samharamurti: Śiva in
Elephant-Killing Aspect.* Granite.
South India, Chola Period, 11th
century. H. 72.4 cm.  62.164

299

*Śiva and Parvati: Uma-Sahitamurti.*
Copper. South India, early Chola
Period, early 10th century.
H. 103.5 cm. 61.94

*Śiva and Parvati: Alingana-*
*Chandrasekharamurti.* Copper. South
India, Chola Period, 11th-12th
century. H. 34 cm. 54.7

*Nataraja: Śiva as King of Dance.*
Copper. South India, Chola Period,
11th century. H. 111.5 cm. 30.331

*Vinadharamurti: Śiva as King of*
*Music.* Bronze. South India, Chola
Period, ca. 1000. H. 76 cm. 71.117

*Śiva's Trident with Ardhanarisvara:*
*Half-Śiva/Half-Parvati.* Bronze.
South India, Chola Period, 11th-12th
century. H. 35.5 cm. 69.117

*Ganesha: Elephant-Headed God,*
*Remover of Obstacles.* Bronze.
South India, Chola Period,
12th century. H. 50.2 cm. 70.62

300

*Śaiva Saint, Manikkavachakar.*
Bronze. South India, 12th-13th
century. H. 33.5 cm. 67.148

*Narasimha: Lion Incarnation of
Vishnu.* Bronze. South India, Chola
Period, ca. 13th century.
H. 55.3 cm. 73.187

*A Guardian of Śiva.* Stone. India,
Mysore, Hoysala Dynasty, 12th
century. H. 113.4 cm. 64.369

301

*Ravana Shaking Mount Kailasa.*
Sandstone. Central India, 8th
century. H. 139.1 cm. 71.173

*Mithuna: Loving Couple.* Sandstone.
India, Rajasthan, from the Purana
Mahadeva Temple (dated 973),
Harsagiri. H. 35.3 cm. 62.165

*Salabhanjika: Female Deity with a
Tree.* India, Rajasthan, from the
Purana Mahadeva Temple (dated 973),
Harsagiri. H. 54.6 cm. 67.202

*Frieze of Musicians and Dancer.* Sandstone. India, Rajasthan, from
the Purana Mahadeva Temple (dated 973), Harsagiri. W. 95.3 cm. 69.34

*Dancing Ganesha.* Red sandstone. India, Khajuraho region, 1000. H. 61.3 cm. 61.93

*Stele with the Twenty-Third Jain Tirthankara, Parśvanatha.* Sandstone. Central India, 9th century. H. 160.7 cm. 61.419

*Vidyadevi: The Jain Goddess of Learning.* White marble. India, Western Rajasthan, 10th-11th century. H. 106.7 cm. 72.152

*King Parikshit and Rishis.* Page from the *Bhagavata Purana.* Color on paper. India, Rajasthan, Mewar School, ca. 1575. H. 22.8 cm. 60.53

Page from the Issarda series of the *Bhagavata Purana.* Color on paper. India, Rajasthan, Mewar School, ca. 1575. W. 25.7 cm. 71.234

*Poet-Musician,* folio 110v from the *Tuti-nama* (manuscript almost complete). Color and gold on paper. India, Mughal School, reign of Akbar, ca. 1560. H. 20.3 cm. 62.279

*Alam Shah Closing the Dam at Shishan Pass.* Page from *Dastan-i-Amir Hamza.* Color and gold on muslin. India, Mughal School, reign of Akbar, ca. 1570. H. 64.8 cm. 76.74

304

*A Young Ascetic Walking by the Bank of a River.* Color on paper. Attributed to Basawan, Indian, Mughal School, ca. 1560. H. 38.9 cm. 67.244

*Page from a* Razm Nama (Book of Wars). Dated 1616. Color on paper. India, Mughal School. H. 35.5 cm. 60.44

*Siege of Arbela.* Color and gold on paper. Designed by Basawan, painted by Sur Gujarati, Indian, Mughal School, late 16th century. H. 38.7 cm. 47.502

Page from *Ta'rikh-i-alfi (History of a Thousand Years).* Color on paper. India, Mughal School, late 16th century. H. 42.3 cm. 32.36

*Humuyan's Victory over the Afghans.* Page from the *Akbar Nama.* Color on paper. India, Mughal School, reign of Akbar, ca. 1600. H. 31.1 cm. 71.77

*Portrait of Akbar.* Grisaille. India, Mughal School, early 17th century. H. 25.4 cm. 71.78

305

*Prince Visiting a Hermitage.* Color on paper. India, Mughal School, reign of Shah Jahan, ca. 1635. H. 37.5 cm. 71.79

*Imperial Rooster.* Color on paper. Signed: Dilaram Padarat Kashmiri. India, Mughal School, early 17th century. H. 18.3 cm. 44.501

*Hunting Scene.* Color on paper. India, Mughal School, early 17th century. H. 37.2 cm. 39.66

*Nayika Madhya Dhira Adhira.* Page from Bhanu Datta's *Rasamanjari.* Color on paper. India, Rajasthan, Mewar School, ca. 1630. H. 25.4 cm. 60.52

*Krishna.* Page from the *Rasikapriya.* Dated 1634. Color on paper. India, Malwa School. H. 20.8 cm. 38.303

*Ragini Madhu Madhavi.* Color on
paper. India, Malwa School,
ca. 1660. H. 20 cm.  25.1336

*Ragini Kedara.* Color on paper.
India, Malwa School, ca. 1680.
H. 20.3 cm.  60.116

*Gandi Ragini.* Color on paper. India,
Malwa School, ca. 1750. H. 30.8 cm.
68.109

*Ragini Pancham.* Color on paper.
India, Rajasthan, Mewar School,
mid-17th century. H. 38 cm.  31.451

*Kakubha Ragini.* Color on paper.
India, Raghugarh School, ca. 1780.
H. 20.5 cm.  75.40

307

*Radha and Krishna.* Page from Bhanu Datta's *Rasamanjari.*
Color on paper. India, Punjab Hills, Basohli School,
ca. 1695. H. 23.3 cm. 65.249

*Visvamitra.* Color on paper. India,
Punjab Hills, Basohli School,
ca. 1700. H. 20 cm. 66.27

*Śiva and Parvati Seated on an
Elephant Skin.* Color on paper.
India, Punjab Hills, Basohli School,
ca. 1700. H. 23.2 cm. 52.587

*Palace Ladies Hunting from a
Pavilion.* Color and gold on paper.
India, Rajasthan, Kotah School,
ca. 1760-1770. H. 38.1 cm. 55.48

308

*Durga Slaying Mahisha.* Color on paper. India, Punjab
Hills, Basohli School, ca. 1700. W. 23.5 cm. 60.51

*Angry Heroine.* Page from Bhanu Datta's *Rasamanjari.*
India, Nurpur School, ca. 1710. W. 28.3 cm. 67.239

*Bitch with Litter.* Color on paper. India, Rajasthan,
Bikaner School, ca. 1700. W. 25.3 cm. 69.77

309

*Krishna Awaiting Radha.* Color on paper. India, Punjab Hills, Guler School, ca. 1760. H. 18.2 cm. 36.685

*Hindola Raga.* Color on paper. India, Punjab Hills, Guler School, ca. 1790. H. 20.7 cm. 75.9

*The Child Krishna Crying for the Moon.* Color on paper. India, Punjab Hills, Guler School, ca. 1790. H. 24.1 cm. 71.80

*Krishna and Radha Watching Rain Clouds: Rainy Season from the Baramasa Series.* Color on paper. India, Punjab Hills, Kangra School, ca. 1790. H. 21 cm. 73.104

*Durga Slaying Mahisha.* Color on paper. India, Punjab Hills, Kangra School, late 18th century. W. 27.5 cm. 55.667

311

*Toilette of Radha.* Color and gold on paper. India, Punjab Hills, Kangra School, early 19th century. H. 23.2 cm. 53.245

*Worship of Śri Natha-ji.* Temple hanging (*pacchavai*), color on cloth. India, Rajasthan, Nathadwara School, early 19th century. H. 206 cm. 37.454

*Textile.* Lampas weave, silk. India, Jaipur School, 17th century. Over-all: W. 1 m. 72.5 cm. Detail: H. 92.7 cm. 53.474

*Pendant: Krishna with Devotees.* Gold with enamel in *champlevé* technique. India, Rajasthan, 17th-18th century. H. 5.1 cm. 46.257

*Millefleur Carpet.* Senna knot, silk and wool. India, Mughal School, early 17th century. Over-all: H. 2 m. 92.7 cm. Detail: H. 1 m. 19.5 cm. 36.17

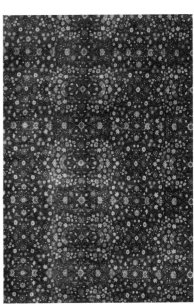

312

*Panels from a Box.* Ivory. India,
Mughal School, Northeast Deccan,
ca. 1700. W. 30.3 cm. 69.229

*Hookah Bottle.* Blue glass with gold.
India, Mughal School, ca. 1700.
H. 7-3/4 inches. 61.44

*Notes*

# Southeast Asian Art

316

*Krishna Govardhana.* Gray limestone.
Cambodia, Phnom Da, Pre-Angkorean
Period, 1st half 6th century.
H. 118.8 cm. 73.106

*Head of Buddha.* Bluish-gray
sandstone. Cambodia, probably from
Angkor Borei, Pre-Angkorean Period,
7th century. H. 25.4 cm. 32.43

*Vishnu.* Gray sandstone. Cambodia,
Pre-Angkorean Period, style of
Prasat Andet, 2nd half 7th century.
H. 87 cm. 42.562

*Maitreya: The Buddha of the Future.*
Bronze. Cambodia, Pre-Angkorean
Period, 7th century. H. 28 cm.
72.7

*Head of a Female.* Sandstone.
Cambodia, Pre-Angkorean Period,
early 8th century. H. 26 cm. 70.11

317

*Standing Buddha.* Slate. Thailand. Mon-Dvaravati Period, 7th-8th century. H. 135.3 cm. 73.15

*Buddha with Hands in Gesture of Teaching, Vitarka Mudra.* Bronze. Thailand, Mon-Dvaravati Period, 7th century. H. 21 cm. 58.334

*Votive Plaque with Vishnu.* Gold repoussé. Thailand, Sri Deb, Mon-Dvaravati Period, 7th-8th century. H. 7.6 cm. 73.75

*Rakshasa.* Gray sandstone. Cambodia, Koh Ker style, 2nd quarter of 10th century. H. 70 cm. 67.146

*Standing Ashura.* Bronze. Cambodia, Koh Ker style, 2nd quarter of 10th century. H. 17.7 cm. 72.221

*Torso of a Female Deity.* Sandstone. Cambodia, Bakheng style, late 9th-early 10th century. H. 88.9 cm. 71.134

*Lintel with Garuda.* Sandstone. Cambodia, Preah Ko style, late 9th century. W. 118 cm. 67.37

*Head of Śiva.* Tan sandstone. Cambodia, Koh Ker style, reign of Jayavarman IV, 928-941. H. 41.9 cm. 40.53

*Buddha Sheltered by Mucalinda, the Serpent King.* Bronze. Cambodia, Angkor Wat style, early 12th century. H. 58.4 cm. 63.263

*Śiva.* Gray sandstone. Cambodia, Baphnon style, 1st half 11th century. H. 76.5 cm. 41.25

319

*Buddha Enthroned.* Bronze. Cambodia, Angkor Wat style, 1st half 12th century. H. 26.7 cm. 42.149

*Finial with the Temptation of Buddha by Mara.* Bronze. Cambodia, Bayon style, late 12th-early 13th century. H. 39.2 cm. 64.93

*Female Figure.* Sandstone. Cambodia, late Baphnon style, 3rd quarter 11th century. H. 91.4 cm. 70.60

*Relief of an Apsara.* Sandstone. Cambodia, Angkor Thom, possibly from the Terrace of the Leper King, late 12th-early 13th century. H. 61 cm. 38.304

*Head of Lokesvara.* Pink sandstone. Cambodia, Bayon style, late 12th-early 13th century. H. 35.3 cm. 55.47

320

*Frieze with Apsaras.* Sandstone. Cambodia, Bayon style,
late 12th-early 13th century. H. 87.7 cm. 38.433

*Śiva.* Sandstone. Viet Nam, Champa,
from Dong-duong, Indrapura, 9th
century. H. 86.3 cm. 35.147

*Head of Buddha.* Volcanic stone.
Java, from Borobudur, early 9th
century. H. 30.5 cm. 42.1087

321

*Bracket with Kala Mask.* Volcanic
stone. Java, ca. 12th-14th
century. H. 40 cm.  75.104

*Notes*

Ch'inese Art

324

*Jar.* Earthenware with slip painting. China, Yang-shao Culture, type-site Pan-shan, Kansu Province, Neolithic Period, ca. 2500-2000 BC. H. 36.2 cm. 30.332

*Yüeh: Tanged Axe.* Bronze. China, Shang Dynasty, 13th-11th century BC. H. 21.1 cm. 37.27

*Ku: Beaker.* Bronze. China, Shang Dynasty, 13th-12th century BC. H. 26.8 cm. 60.43

*Ting: Tripod Cauldron.* Bronze. China, probably An-yang, Honan Province, Shang Dynasty, 11th century BC. H. 24.5 cm. 62.281

*Fang-yu: Square Bucket.* Bronze. China, probably An-yang, Honan Province, Shang Dynasty, 12th-11th century BC. H. 26.7 cm. 63.103

*Hsien: Steamer.* Bronze. China, Shang Dynasty, ca. 1100 BC. H. 39.4 cm. 75.96

*T'ao-t'ieh Mask.* Marble. China, probably An-yang, Honan Province, Shang Dynasty, 13th-11th century BC. W. 13.3 cm. 52.585

*Composite Feline-Bovine-Elephant Head.* Jade (nephrite). China, probably An-yang, Honan Province, Shang Dynasty, ca. 1200-1100 BC. L. 4.2 cm. 52.573

*Tsun: Vase.* Bronze. China, Western Chou Dynasty, 11th-10th century BC. H. 29.5 cm. 51.151

*Li-ting: Hollow-Legged Tripod Cauldron.* Bronze. China, reportedly Sian, Shensi Province, Western Chou Dynasty, ca. 950-900 BC. D. 27.1 cm. 61.203

*Kuei: Handled Bowl on Rectangular Plinth.* Bronze. China, Eastern Chou Dynasty, Spring and Autumn Period, 7th-6th century BC. H. 34.3 cm. 74.73

326

*Elongated Hu: Flask.* Bronze.
China, Western Chou Dynasty, ca.
10th century BC. H. 46.3 cm.  44.61

*Po: Bell.* Bronze. China, probably
Shansi Province, Eastern Chou
Dynasty, Warring States Period,
early 5th century BC. H. 41.3 cm.
62.44

*Openwork Plaque with Intertwined
Dragons and Birds.* Jade (nephrite).
China, Eastern Chou Dynasty, Warring
States Period, 480-221 BC.
W. 7.5 cm.  52.584

*Shaft Mounting.* Bronze with silver,
gold, speculum inlays. China,
Chin-ts'un, Honan Province, Eastern
Chou Dynasty, Warring States Period,
ca. 400-200 BC. H. 13.5 cm.  30.730

*"Hunting" Hu: Jar with Pictorial
Relief.* Bronze. China, Eastern Chou
Dynasty, late Spring and Autumn-
early Warring States Period, ca.
5th century BC. H. 25.5 cm.  75.62

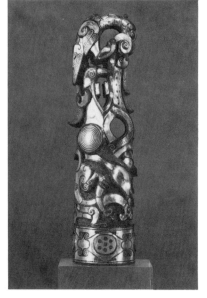

327

*Cranes and Serpents.* Lacquered wood. China, Ch'ang-sha, Hunan Province, Eastern Chou Dynasty, Warring States Period, State of Ch'u, ca. 4th-3rd century BC. H. 132.1 cm. 38.9

*The Kill.* One of a pair of shells, painting over carved design. China, late Eastern Chou Dynasty, Warring States Period or early Western Han Dynasty, 3rd-2nd century BC. W. 8.9 cm. 57.139

*Panel from Tomb Chamber.* Stone with carved relief. China, probably Szechwan Province, Han Dynasty, 206 BC-AD 220. H. 120 cm. 62.280

*Lien* or *Chung: Cylindrical Box.* Earthenware with molded relief under lead glaze. China, probably Shensi Province, Han Dynasty, 206 BC-AD 220. H. 26.7 cm. 48.214

*Vase with Peaked Lid.* Earthenware with molded relief under lead glaze. China, Han Dynasty, 206 BC-AD 220. H. 47 cm. 24.196

328

*Vase.* Stoneware with incised and
applied relief under iron glaze.
China, late Western Han-early Eastern
Han Dynasty, ca. 1st century BC-
AD 1st century. H. 45.7 cm. 54.370

*P'u-shou: Monster-Headed Door Ring Holder.* Gilt bronze.
China, reportedly Honan Province, Six Dynasties Period,
ca. mid-6th century. W. 20 cm. 30.371

*Top of a Hun-p'ing: Urn of the Soul.*
Stoneware with iron glaze, Yüeh type.
China, probably Shao-hsing region,
Chekiang Province, Six Dynasties
Period, Wu or Western Chin Dynasty,
3rd century. D. 21.6 cm. 60.76

*Kulan (Wild Ass): Pole Top.* Bronze.
China, Inner Mongolia, Ordos steppe
region, ca. 2nd century. H. 17.8 cm.
62.46

*Panels from Funerary Model of a Cooking Stove.*
Earthenware with die-stamped relief. China, Eastern Han
Dynasty, ca. 2nd-3rd century. W. 27.3 cm.
25.134, 25.135

*Hollow Tile from Tomb Chamber Wall.* Earthenware with
die-stamped relief. China, Eastern Han Dynasty,
AD 25-220. W. 105.4 cm. 15.70

*Caparisoned Horse.* Earthenware with
polychrome painting. China, Six
Dynasties Period, Northern Wei
Dynasty, ca. 525. H. 22.2 cm. 29.985

*Stele: Maitreya and Attendants.*
Dated 500. Sandstone. China, Six
Dynasties Period, Northern Wei
Dynasty. H. 94.6 cm. 59.130

*Head of Bodhisattva Kuan-yin.*
Limestone. China, probably Lung-men
caves, Honan Province, Six Dynasties
Period, Northern Wei Dynasty,
ca. 510-520. H. 36.2 cm. 15.77

330

*Stele: Sakyamuni Trinity.* Dated 537. Limestone. China, Six Dynasties Period, Eastern Wei Dynasty. H. 77.5 cm.  14.567

*Stele: Maitreya as the Future Buddha.* Marble. China, Six Dynasties Period, Northern Ch'i Dynasty, 550-577. H. 86.3 cm.  17.320

*Seated Sakyamuni Buddha.* Limestone. China, Sui Dynasty, ca. 590-620. H. 51.4 cm.  64.152

*Squatting Caryatid Monster.* Limestone. China, Hsiang-t'ang-shan (northern caves), Honan Province, Six Dynasties Period, Northern Ch'i Dynasty, ca. 570. H. 74.9 cm.  57.360

*Bodhisattva Kuan-yin.* Sandstone with polychromy. China, late Six Dynasties Period, Northern Ch'i Dynasty or early Sui Dynasty, 575-600. H. 138.8 cm.  62.162

331

*Guardian Lion.* Marble. China,
early T'ang Dynasty, 7th century.
H. 78.7 cm. 65.473

*Candlestick.* Cream-glazed stoneware.
China, northern, Sui or early T'ang
Dynasty, ca. 7th century. H. 29.8 cm.
30.322

*Sakyamuni Triad: Buddha Attended by
Manjuśri and Samantabhadra.* Hanging
scroll, color on silk. China, T'ang
Dynasty, ca. 900. H. 94 cm. 75.92

*Camel.* Amber lead-glazed earthenware.
China, T'ang Dynasty, ca. late 7th-
8th century. H. 80 cm. 67.147

*Jar.* Earthenware with applied relief
and three-color *(san-ts'ai)* lead
glazes. China, T.ang Dynasty, ca.
late 7th-8th century. H. 13 cm.
40.44

*Caparisoned Horse.* Earthenware with
applied relief and three-color
*(san-ts'ai)* lead glazes. China,
T'ang Dynasty, ca. late 7th-8th
century. H. 76.8 cm. 55.295

332

*Jar.* Cream-glazed stoneware. China, northern, early T'ang Dynasty, ca. 7th century. H. 27.6 cm. 30.323

*Bull.* Painted earthenware. China, T'ang Dynasty, 618-907. H. 16.2 cm. 29.987

*Harpist.* Earthenware with three-color *(san-ts'ai)* lead glazes. China, T'ang Dynasty, 618-907. H. 32.1 cm. 31.450

*Stem Cup.* Beaten silver, chased and parcel-gilt design on ringmatted ground. China, T'ang Dynasty, ca. 8th century. H. 8.9 cm. 51.396

*Panel from Sarcophagus.* Incised stone. China, early T'ang Dynasty, ca. mid-7th-early 8th century. H. 119.4 cm. 75.63

*Platter on Three Feet.* Beaten silver with chased and parcel gilt design on ringmatted ground. China, T'ang Dynasty, ca. 8th century. H. 8.9 cm. 72.39

*Lien* or *Chung: Covered Cylindrical Box.* Gilt bronze with openwork and chased design. China, Sui-early T'ang Dynasty, late 6th-early 7th century. H. 17.2 cm. 72.44

*Mirror.* Bronze with beaten gold and silver sheets inlaid in lacquer ground (*p'ing t'o* technique). China, T'ang Dynasty, ca. 8th century. D. 19.2 cm. 73.74

*Bodhisattva Kuan-yin.* Dated 687. Limestone with traces of polychromy. China, reportedly Pai-ma-ssu (temple), Loyang, Honan Province, T'ang Dynasty. H. 170.8 cm. 66.364

*Torso: Bodhisattva Kuan-yin.* Marble. China, reportedly Ling-yen-ssu (temple), Lung-yen-shan, Pao-ting, Hopei Province, T'ang Dynasty, 8th century. H. 177.8 cm. 29.981

*Eleven-Headed Kuan-yin.* Sandstone. China, T'ang Dynasty, 1st quarter 8th century. H. 129.5 cm. 59.129

334

*Eleven-Headed Kuan-yin.* Wood. China, T'ang Dynasty, late 7th century. H. 62.8 cm. 70.66

*Textile.* Patterned weave, silk. China, 8th century. H. 26.8 cm. 54.109

*Attendant of Manjusri (?).* Hollow dry lacquer. China, late T'ang Dynasty or early Five Dynasties Period, 9th-10th century. H. 40 cm. 53.356

*Ewer in Form of a Sheng Player.* Stoneware, slip-coated with underglaze painting. China, northern, Liao Dynasty, ca. 11th century. H. 21.3 cm. 53.248

*Jar.* Porcelain, incised and impressed under white glaze. China, northern, Liao Dynasty, 10th-11th century. H. 12.7 cm. 57.29

*Seated Amitabha Buddha.* Gilt bronze. China, Liao Dynasty, 10th century. H. 22.8 cm. 42.1082

*Potala (Water and Moon) Kuan-yin.* Wood (loquat). China, Five Dynasties Period, 10th century. H. 15.1 cm. 65.556

*Bodhisattva Kuan-yin.* Gilt bronze. China, Liao Dynasty, 10th century. H. 43.8 cm. 76.14

*Taoist Figure.* Wood (loquat) and ivory. China, Southern Sung Dynasty, 1127-1279. H. 31.8 cm. 64.368

*Bodhisattva.* Wood (cypress). China, Chin Dynasty, 13th century. H. 46 cm. 63.581

336

*Petal-Rimmed Baluster Vase.*
Tz'u-chou ware, stoneware. China,
Sung Dynasty, 960-1279, or earlier.
H. 32.1 cm. 42.656

*Phoenix-Headed Ewer.* Ch'ing-pai ware,
porcelain. China, Five Dynasties
Period or Northern Sung Dynasty,
10th-11th century. H. 38.7 cm.
65.468

*Baluster Vase.* Tz'u-chou ware,
"Chiao-tso" type, stoneware. China,
probably Honan Province, Northern
Sung Dynasty, 10th-11th century.
H. 41.2 cm. 48.226

*Ewer.* Tz'u-chou ware, Teng-feng
type, stoneware. China, probably
Honan Province, Sung Dynasty,
960-1279. H. 17.5 cm. 48.219

*Jar.* Tz'u-chou ware, stoneware.
China, Sung Dynasty, 960-1279.
H. 34.9 cm. 48.225

*Mei-p'ing: Gallipot Vase.* Tz'u-chou
ware, stoneware. China, Northern
Sung Dynasty, 960-1127. H. 34.3 cm.
40.52

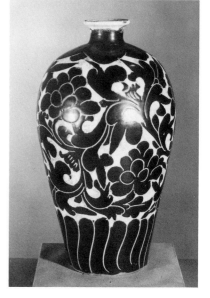

*Circular Covered Box.* Ting ware, porcelain. China, Northern Sung Dynasty, 960-1127. D. 10.5 cm. 57.32

*Circular Covered Box.* Northern Celadon, Yao-chou type, stoneware. China, probably Shensi Province, Northern Sung Dynasty, 960-1127. D. 10.7 cm. 62.41

*Ewer.* "Tung ware" (or Northern Celadon of Yao-chou type ?), stoneware. China, Northern Sung Dynasty, 960-1127. H. 18.7 cm. 48.220

*Lion: Incense-Burner Top.* Northern Celadon, stoneware. China, Northern Sung Dynasty, ca. 12th century. H. 18.4 cm. 66.26

338

*Circular Brush Washer.* Ju ware, stoneware. China, Lin-ju Hsien, Honan Province, Northern Sung Dynasty, late 11th-early 12th century. D. 12.8 cm. 57.40

*Plate.* Chün ware, stoneware. China, Northern Sung Dynasty, 960-1127. D. 18.1 cm. 42.665

*Shallow Bowl with Fluted Well and Foliate Rim.* Chün ware, stoneware. China, probably Honan Province, 13th-14th century. D. 23.5 cm. 57.33

*Ting: Tripod.* Lung-ch'üan ware, porcelain. China, Chekiang Province, Southern Sung Dynasty, 1127-1279. D. 13.9 cm. 54.790

*Ch'a-tou: Vase in Shape of a Grain Measure.* Lung-ch'üan ware, porcelain. China, Chekiang Province, Southern Sung Dynasty, 1127-1279. D. 15.6 cm. 57.73

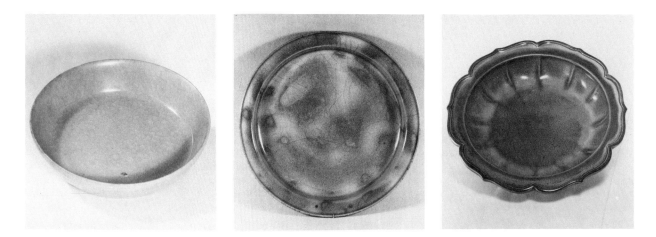

339

*Mallow-Petal Bowl.* Kuan ware, porcelain. China, southern, Southern Sung Dynasty, 1127-1279. D. 17.5 cm. 57.66

*Lu: Incense Burner.* Kuan ware, porcelain. China, southern, Southern Sung Dynasty, 1127-1279. W. 15.5 cm. 57.63

*Washer Basin.* Kuan ware, porcelain with copper rim. China, southern, Southern Sung Dynasty, 1127-1279. D. 24.2 cm. 57.48

*Ladies of the Court* (detail). After a painting by Chou Wen-chü of the 10th century. Handscroll, ink and slight color on silk. China, Sung Dynasty, datable before 1140. W. 168.5 cm. 76.1

*Buddhist Retreat by Stream and Mountains.* Hanging scroll, ink on silk. Attributed to Chü-jan, Chinese, active ca. 960-980, Northern Sung Dynasty. H. 185.4 cm. 59.348

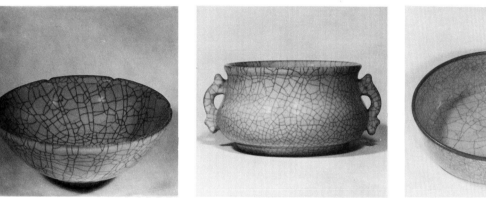

*Barbarian Royalty Worshipping Buddha.* Handscroll, ink and color on silk.
Attributed to Chao Kuang-fu, Chinese, active 960-975, Northern Sung Dynasty.
W. 103 cm. 57.358

*Palace Landscape.* Album leaf, ink and color on silk.
China, Northern Sung Dynasty, 11th century. W. 40.7 cm.
71.40

*Frontispiece Illustration for Lotus Sutra* (detail). Handscroll,
gold ink on paper. China, Sung Dynasty, 960-1279.
W. 78.7 cm. 70.64

*Ch'i-shan wu chin: Streams and Mountains without End* (detail). Handscroll, ink and slight color on silk. China, Northern Sung Dynasty, early 12th century. W. 213 cm. 53.126

*Cloudy Mountains* (detail). Dated 1130. Handscroll, ink and slight color on silk. Mi Yu-jen, Chinese, 1072-1151, Southern Sung Dynasty. W. 194.3 cm. 33.220

*Bamboo and Ducks by a Rushing Stream.* Hanging scroll, ink and light color on silk. Ma Yüan, Chinese, active ca. 1190-ca. 1224, Southern Sung Dynasty. H. 61 cm. 67.145

*Cottages in a Misty Grove in Autumn.* Dated 1117. Album leaf, ink and color on silk. Li An-chung, Chinese, active ca. 1115-1140, Northern Sung Dynasty. H. 27 cm. 63.588

342

*Birds in a Grove in a Mountainous
Landscape in Winter.* Hanging scroll,
ink and slight color on silk.
Kao Tao (?), Chinese, Sung Dynasty,
12th century. H. 170 cm. 66.115

*The Knick-Knack Peddler.* Dated 1201. Album leaf, ink and
slight color on silk. Li Sung, Chinese, active ca. 1190-
1230, Southern Sung Dynasty. H. 24.2 cm. 63.582

*Scholar Reclining and Watching Rising Clouds.* Dated 1256.
Fan painting, ink and slight color on silk. Ma Lin,
Chinese, active mid-13th century, Southern Sung Dynasty.
H. 25.3 cm. 61.421

*Sakyamuni Coming Down from the Mountains.* Dated 1244. Hanging scroll, ink on paper. China, Southern Sung Dynasty. H. 74.6 cm. 70.2

*The Football Players.* Hanging scroll, ink and light color on silk. China, late Southern Sung or early Yüan Dynasty, ca. 1250-1350. H. 115.6 cm. 71.26

*Bodhisattva Samantabhadra.* Hanging scroll, ink and color on silk. China, Southern Sung Dynasty, 1127-1279. H. 110.8 cm. 62.161

*Seated Arhat with Two Attendants.* Hanging scroll, ink and color on silk. China, Southern Sung Dynasty, 1127-1279. H. 93.7 cm. 76.91

*Tiger* (one of a pair). Hanging scroll, ink on silk. Attributed to Mu Ch'i, Chinese, 1177-1239, Southern Sung Dynasty. H. 128.3 cm. 58.428

*White-Robed Kuan-yin.* Hanging scroll, ink on paper. China (or Japan?), early 14th century. H. 104 cm. 72.160

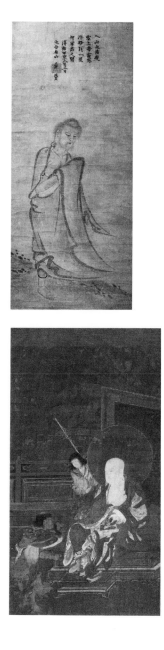

*A Prunus in the Moonlight.* Hanging scroll, ink on silk. Wang Mien, Chinese, 1287-1366, Yüan Dynasty. H. 164.5 cm. 74.26

*Peonies.* Hanging scroll, ink and color on silk. China, Yüan Dynasty, 1279-1368. H. 145.4 cm. 76.90

*Raft-Cup with Taoist Immortal.* Dated 1345. Cast silver with engraving. Chu Pi-shan, Chinese, ca. 1300-ca. 1362, Yüan Dynasty. L. 20.5 cm. 77.7

*Jar.* Tz'u-chou ware, stoneware. China, Yüan Dynasty, 1279-1368. H. 27.9 cm. 48.215

*Bowl with Taoist Designs.* White jade (nephrite). China, Yüan Dynasty, late 13th-early 14th century. W. 15.9 cm. 52.510

*Jar with Lion-Head Handles.* Porcelain painted in underglaze blue. China, Yüan Dynasty, 14th century. H. 39.3 cm. 62.154

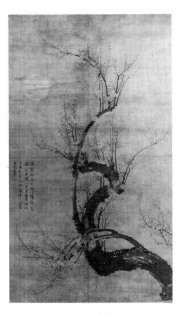

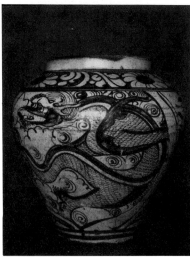

*Plate with Peony Design.* Carved cinnabar lacquer on wood. Yang Mao, Chinese, Yüan Dynasty, late 14th-early 15th century. D. 16.5 cm. 77.6

*Plate with Dragon Among Clouds.* Lung-ch'üan type, porcelain with biscuit relief floated on celadon glaze. China, Yüan Dynasty, 14th century. D. 43.2 cm. 61.92

*Sakyamuni as an Ascetic.* Gilt bronze. China, Yüan Dynasty, early 14th century. H. 44.2 cm. 66.116

*The Lantern Night Excursion of Chung K'uei* (detail). Handscroll, ink on silk. Yen Hui, Chinese, first half 14th century, Yüan Dynasty. W. 240.3 cm. 61.206

*The Second Coming of the Fifth Patriarch.* Part of handscroll mounted as hanging scroll, ink on paper. Yin-t'o-lo (Indara), Chinese, active ca. mid-14th century. Yüan Dynasty. W. 45.5 cm. 67.211

346

*Three Horses and Four Grooms*
(detail). Handscroll, ink and color
on silk. Jen Jen-fa, Chinese,
1254-1327, early Yüan Dynasty.
W. 136.8 cm. 60.181

*Ink Flowers* (detail). Dated 1361.
Handscroll, ink on paper. Chao
Chung, Chinese, active ca. 2nd half
14th century, Yüan Dynasty.
W. 153.2 cm. 67.36

*Bamboos, Rocks, and Lonely Orchids.*
(detail). Handscroll, ink on paper.
Chao Meng-fu, Chinese, 1254-1322,
Yüan Dynasty. W. 144.2 cm. 63.515

*Chiu-k'o-t'u: The Nine Songs* (detail).
Handscroll, ink on paper. Chang Wu,
Chinese, active 1335-1365, Yüan
Dynasty. W. 438.2 cm. 59.138

*Bodhidharma Crossing the Yangtze
on a Reed.* Hanging scroll, ink on
paper. China, Yüan Dynasty, 1279-
1368. H. 89.2 cm. 64.44

*Old Trees by a Cool Spring.* Dated
1326. Hanging scroll, ink on silk.
Li Shih-hsing, Chinese, 1282-1328,
Yüan Dynasty. H. 165.7 cm. 70.41

*Poetic Feeling in a Thatched Pavilion* (detail). Dated
1347. Handscroll, ink on paper. Wu Chen, Chinese,
1280-1354. W. 99.4 cm. 63.259

*Leisure Enough to Spare.* Dated 1360. Handscroll, ink
on paper. Yao T'ing-mei, Chinese, active 14th century,
Yüan Dynasty. W. 84 cm. 54.791

*Lily and Butterflies.* Hanging scroll,
ink on silk. Liu Shan-shou, Chinese,
Yüan Dynasty, 14th century.
H. 160 cm. 71.132

*Taoist Immortal, Chung-li Ch'üan.*
Hanging scroll, ink and color on
silk. Chao Ch'i, Chinese, late Yüan-
early Ming Dynasty, 14th century.
H. 134.5 cm. 76.13

*Landscape in Blue-and-Green Style* (detail). Handscroll, ink and color on silk. Shih-jui, Chinese, active ca. 1425-1469, Ming Dynasty. W. 170.2 cm. 73.72

*Hundred Birds Admiring the Peacocks.* Hanging scroll, ink and color on silk. Yin Hung, Chinese, Ming Dynasty, late 15th-early 16th century. H. 240 cm. 74.31

*Yaksha Generals* (one of a pair). Hanging scroll, color on silk. China, Ming Dynasty. H. 227.2 cm. 73.71

*River Village in a Rainstorm.* Hanging scroll, ink and slight color on silk. Lü Wen-ying, Chinese, active late 15th century. H. 169.2 cm. 70.76

*The Hermit Hsü Yu Resting by a Stream.* Hanging scroll, ink and slight color on silk. Tai Chin, Chinese, 1388-1462, Ming Dynasty. H. 138 cm. 74.45

349

*Part of a Screen Panel.*
Tapestry, silk and metallic
threads. China, Ming Dynasty
(1368-1644). H. 198.2 cm. 16.1334

*Chrysanthemums and Cabbage* (detail). Dated 1490. Handscroll, ink and slight
color on paper. T'ao Cheng, Chinese, active 1480-1532, Ming Dynasty.
W. 151.7 cm. 60.40

*The Poet Lin P'u Wandering in the
Moonlight.* Hanging scroll, ink and
slight color on paper. Tu Chin,
Chinese, active ca. 1465-1487, Ming
Dynasty. H. 156.5 cm. 54.582

*A Distant View of Tiger Hill* (from *Twelve Views of
Tiger Hill, Suchou*). Album leaf, ink on paper. Shen Chou,
Chinese, 1427-1509, Ming Dynasty. W. 40.2 cm. 64.371

350

*Old Pine Tree.* Handscroll, ink on paper. Wen Cheng-ming, Chinese, 1470-1559,
Ming Dynasty. W. 138.8 cm. 64.43

*Ink Prunus.* Hanging scroll, ink on
silk. Peng Hsü, Chinese, active ca.
1488-1521, Ming Dynasty. H. 127 cm.
70.80

*Beggars and Street Characters* (detail). Dated 1516.
Handscroll, ink and color on paper. Chou Ch'en, Chinese,
active ca. 1500-1535, Ming Dynasty. W. 244.5 cm. 64.94

*Clouds and Waves in the Yangtze
Gorge of Mu-shan.* Hanging scroll,
ink and light color on paper.
Hsieh Shih-ch'en, Chinese, 1487-
after 1567, Ming Dynasty.
H. 241.9 cm. 68.213

*Scholar-Hermits in Stream and Mountain* (detail).
Handscroll, ink and light color on silk. T'ang Yin,
Chinese, 1470-1523, Ming Dynasty. W. 232.4 cm. 76.94

*The Five Hundred Lohans: Disciples of Buddha* (detail).
Handscroll, ink and color on paper. Wu Pin, Chinese,
active ca. 1567-ca. 1617, Ming Dynasty.
W. 20 m. 74.8 cm. 71.16

*Chao Meng-fu Writing the Heart Sutra in Exchange for Tea*
(detail). Dated 1543. Handscroll, ink and color on paper.
Ch'iu Ying, Chinese, active ca. 1522-1560, Ming Dynasty.
W. 77.8 cm. 63.102

*Mountains on a Clear Autumn Day.* Handscroll, ink on paper. Tung Ch'i-ch'ang, Chinese, 1555-1636, Ming Dynasty. W. 136.8 cm. 59.46

*Chüeh: Tripod Cup.* Porcelain. China, Ming Dynasty, reign of Yung-lo, 1403-1424. H. 15 cm. 57.59

*Greeting the Spring* (detail). Dated 1600. Handscroll, ink and color on paper. Wu Pin, Chinese, active ca. 1567-ca. 1617, Ming Dynasty. W. 245.1 cm. 59.45

*Lady Hsüan-wen Giving Instructions on the Classics.* Dated 1638. Hanging scroll, ink and color on silk. Ch'en Hung-shou, Chinese, 1598-1652, Ming Dynasty. H. 73.7 cm. 61.89

*Wu-hsieh Shan: The Mountain of the Five Cataracts.* Hanging scroll, ink on silk. Ch'en Hung-shou, Chinese, 1598-1652, Ming Dynasty. H. 118.2 cm. 66.366

*Hsü Cheng-yang Moving His Family.* Hanging scroll, ink and color on silk. Ts'ui Tzu-chung, Chinese, died 1644, Ming Dynasty. H. 165.6 cm. 61.90

*Foliate Dish with Grapevines.* Porcelain painted in underglaze blue. China, Ming Dynasty, reign of Hsüan-te, 1426-1435. D. 43.2 cm. 53.127

*Stem Cup with Animals Among Waves.* Porcelain painted in underglaze blue and overglaze red enamel. China, Ming Dynasty, mark and reign of Hsüan-te, 1465-1487. H. 8.9 cm. 57.60

*Bowl with Land of Taoist Immortals.* Porcelain painted in underglaze blue. China, Ming Dynasty, mark and reign of Hsüan-te, 1426-1435. D. 19.2 cm. 62.260

*Bowl with the "Three Friends": Pine, Bamboo, Prunus.* Porcelain painted in underglaze blue. China, Ming Dynasty, mark and reign of Hsüan-te, 1426-1435. D. 30.2 cm. 53.631

354

*Wine Cup with Children in a Landscape.* Porcelain painted in underglaze blue and overglaze red, aubergine, and green enamels, *tou-ts'ai* type. China, Ming Dynasty, mark and reign of Ch'eng-hua, 1465-1487. H. 4.3 cm. 57.61

*Kuan-yin of the South Sea.* Te-hua ware (*blanc de Chine*), porcelain. China, Te-hua Hsien, Fukien Province, late Ming Dynasty, ca. 17th century. H. 45.1 cm. 50.579

*Bowl with Lily Scroll.* Porcelain painted in underglaze blue. China, Ming Dynasty, mark and reign of Ch'eng-hua, 1465-1487. D. 14.5 cm. 67.64

*Covered Jar with Five Elders.* Porcelain painted in underglaze blue and overglaze red, yellow, and green enamels, *wu-ts'ai* type. China, Ming Dynasty, mark and reign of Wan-li, 1573-1619. H. 10.2 cm. 57.62

*Reclining Water Buffalo.* Jade (nephrite). China, Ming Dynasty, 1368-1644. L. 21 cm. 60.282

*Hoop-Backed Armchair, "Lohan type."* Burmese or East Indian rosewood (*huang hua-li*) and woven reed. China, late Ming Dynasty, 17th century. H. 85.4 cm. 55.40

*Mei-p'ing: Vase.* Stoneware with biscuit outline and polychrome glazes, *fa-hua* type. China, probably Ching-te-chen, Kiangsi Province, Ming Dynasty, late 15th century. H. 37 cm. 42.718

*Taoist Immortal, Li T'ieh-kuai.* Bronze. Su Wen-nan, Chinese, Ming Dynasty, 15th century. H. 41.8 cm. 73.158

*Pure Tones of the Hills and Waters* (detail). Dated 1664.
Handscroll, ink and color on paper. Hsiao Yün-ts'ung,
Chinese, 1596-1673, Ch'ing Dynasty. W. 781.2 cm. 54.262

*Fish and Rocks* (detail). Handscroll, ink on paper.
Chu Ta, Chinese, 1624-ca. 1705, Ch'ing Dynasty.
W. 157.5 cm. 53.247

*Morning Sun Over the Mountain of
Heavenly Citadel.* Dated 1614. Hanging
scroll, ink and color on paper.
Ting Yün-p'eng, Chinese, active ca.
1578-1628. H. 212.7 cm. 65.28

*Strolling Companions in the Autumn Mountains.* Double
album leaf mounted as a handscroll, ink and color on
paper. K'un-ts'an, Chinese, active 2nd half 17th century,
Ch'ing Dynasty. W. 64.4 cm. 66.367

357

*Reminiscences of Ch'in-huai River.*
Eight-leaf album, ink and color on
paper. Tao-chi (Shih-t'ao), Chinese,
1641–ca. 1720, Ch'ing Dynasty.
H. 25.5 cm. 66.31

*Landscape in the Style of Tung Yüan
and Chü-jan.* Dated 1650 in inscription
of 1670. Hanging scroll, ink and
white pigment on silk. Kung Hsien,
Chinese, ca. 1620–1689, Ch'ing
Dynasty. H. 216.3 cm. 69.123

*Tall Bamboos and Distant Mountains
After Wang Meng.* Dated 1694.
Hanging scroll, ink on paper. Wang
Hui, Chinese, 1632–1717, Ch'ing
Dynasty. H. 79.4 cm. 53.629

*Album of Landscapes, and Flowers and Birds.* Ten-leaf
album, ink and color on silk. Fan Ch'i, Chinese,
1616–ca. 1695, Ch'ing Dynasty. W. 17.3 cm. 75.22

*Clear Peaks and Blue Sky After Huang Kung-wang* (detail).
Dated 1703–1708. Handscroll, color on paper. Wang
Yüan-ch'i, Chinese, 1642–1715, Ch'ing Dynasty.
W. 267 cm. 72.153

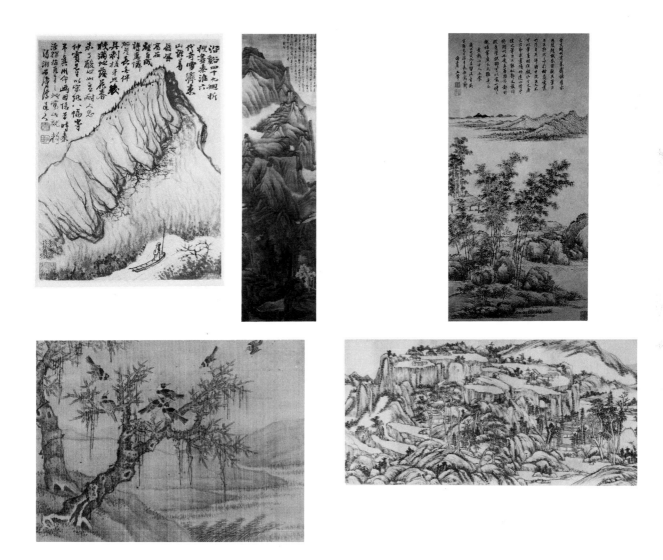

*Landscape After Ni Tsan.* Dated 1707. Hanging scroll, ink and color on paper. Wang Yüan-ch'i, Chinese, 1642-1715, Ch'ing Dynasty. H. 80.3 cm. 54.583

*Portrait of An Ch'i.* Dated 1715. Hanging scroll, ink and color on paper. Wang Hui, T'u Lo, and Yang Chin, Chinese, Ch'ing Dynasty. H. 121.8 cm. 71.17

*Inauguration Portraits of Emperor Ch'ien-lung, the Empress, and the Eleven Imperial Consorts* [titled by the Emperor "A Mind Picture of a Well-Governed and Tranquil Reign"] (detail). Datable to 1737. Handscroll, ink and color on silk. Giuseppe Castiglione (Lang Shih-ning), Italian, 1688-1766, Chinese School, Ch'ing Dynasty. W. 688.3 cm. 69.31

*Conversation in Autumn.* Dated 1732. Hanging scroll, ink and color on paper. Hua Yen, Chinese, 1682-1765, Ch'ing Dynasty. H. 115.3 cm. 54.263

*Drunken Chung K'uei Supported by Ghosts.* Hanging scroll, ink and color on paper. Lo P'ing, Chinese, 1733-1799, Ch'ing Dynasty. H. 96.8 cm. 59.185

*Vase.* Porcelain with peach-bloom glaze. China, Ch'ing Dynasty, mark and reign of K'ang-hsi, 1662-1722. H. 21.1 cm. 42.669

*Baluster Vase.* Porcelain painted in overglaze polychrome enamels, *famille verte* panels on *famille noire.* China, Ch'ing Dynasty, reign of K'ang-Hsi, 1662-1722. H. 44.2 cm. 42.696

*Pi-ch'i-p'ing: Vase.* Lang ware, porcelain with oxblood (*sang-de-boeuf*) glaze. China, Ch'ing Dynasty, reign of K'ang-hsi, 1662-1722. H. 38.1 cm. 44.201

*Vase.* Soft-paste porcelain painted in underglaze blue. China, Ch'ing Dynasty, mark and reign of Yung-cheng, 1723-1735. H. 28.6 cm. 42.728

360

*Vase.* Porcelain painted in overglaze green and black enamels. China, Ch'ing Dynasty, reign of K'ang-hsi, 1662-1722. H. 27.3 cm. 42.685

*Suan-t'ou p'ing: Vase.* Porcelain painted in overglaze polychrome enamels, *Ku yüeh hsüan* style. China, Ch'ing Dynasty, mark and reign of Ch'ien-lung, 1736-1795. H. 19 cm. 71.145

*Vase.* Porcelain painted in overglaze polychrome enamels, *Ku yüeh hsüan* style. China, Ch'ing Dynasty, mark and reign of Ch'ien-lung, 1736-1795. H. 15.4 cm. 63.514

*Vase with Dragon Handles.* Porcelain painted in overglaze polychrome enamels, *Ku yüeh hsüan* style. China, Ch'ing Dynasty, reign of Ch'ien-lung, 1736-1795. H. 27.3 cm. 42.712

*Covered Bowl with T'ao-t'ieh Masks and Ring-Handles.* Jade (jadeite). China, Ch'ing Dynasty, period of Ch'ien-lung, 1736-1795. H. 15.2 cm. 42.620

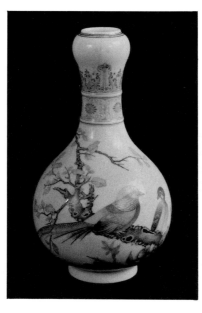

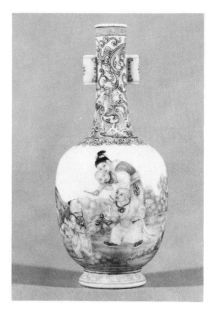

*Notes*

# Korean Art

*Covered Bowl.* Stoneware. Korea, Great Silla Period, 8th-9th c. D. 12 cm. 28.178

*Prunus Vase (maebyong).* Iron-black ware. Korea, Koryo Dynasty, 918-1392. H. 29 cm. 61.270

*Vase.* Celadon. Korea, Koryo Dynasty, 12th-13th century. H. 25.4 cm. 44.164

*Water Jar.* Celadon with inlaid decoration. Korea, Koryo Dynasty, 13th century. H. 30.8 cm. 75.99

*Bottle-Vase with Fish Design. Punch'ong* stoneware. Korea, Yi Dynasty, 15th century. H. 30.5 cm. 62.153

365

*Storage Jar. Punch'ong* stoneware.
Korea, Yi Dynasty, 15th century.
H. 37.5 cm. 63.505

*Bottle.* Stoneware. Korea, Yi
Dynasty, ca. 16th century.
H. 23.3 cm. 69.58

*Amitabha Triad.* Hanging scroll,
ink and color on silk. Korea,
Koryu Period, ca. 1250.
H. 119.1 cm. 61.135

*Notes*

# Japanese Art

*Urn.* Earthenware. Japan, Jomon
Period, ca. 1000 BC. H. 39.4 cm.
60.196

*Haniwa Figure.* Earthenware. Japan,
Tumulus (Kofun) Period, ca. 6th
century. H. 58.4 cm. 62.39

*Dotaku: Bell.* Bronze. Japan, late
Yayoi Period, ca. AD 100-300.
H. 97.8 cm. 16.1102

*Hanka-shiyui-zo: Miroku in
Meditation.* Bronze. Japan, Asuka
Period, 7th century. H. 39.4 cm.
50.86

*Bodhisattva Kannon.* Gilt
bronze. Japan, Hakuho Period,
AD 645-710. H. 33 cm. 50.392

369

*Heavenly Musician.* From Horyu-ji, Nara. Camphor wood with polychromy. Japan, Hakuho Period, AD 645-710. H. 53.7 cm. 54.792

*Woman from an Audience Scene.* Probably from Horyu-ji, Nara. Gray unfired clay. Japan, Hakuho Period, AD 645-710. H. 19 cm. 50.393

*Suikoju: Gigaku Mask.* Paulownia wood, lacquered and painted. Japan, Nara Period, AD 710-784. H. 28 cm. 49.158

*Hand of Buddha.* Wood. Japan, late Nara or early Heian Period, late 8th-early 9th century. H. 40 cm. 56.126

*Nikko: The Sun Bodhisattva.* Carved from one block of Japanese yew. Japan, early Heian Period, ca. AD 800. H. 46.7 cm. 61.48

*Amida's Paradise.* Lacquer on wood, fragment mounted as a box cover. Japan, late Heian Period, ca. 1200. W. 13.2 cm. 61.91

*Processional Mask of a Bosatsu.* Wood with lacquer and paint. Japan, Fujiwara Period, late 12th century. H. 21.9 cm. 50.581

*Shinto Deity, Izu-san Gongen.* Wood. Japan, Kamakura Period, 12th-13th century. H. 100 cm. 54.373

*Enno Gyoja.* Wood. Japan, Kamakura Period, 1183-1333. H. 74.9 cm. 75.65

*Portrait of Hoto Kokushi (Priest Kakushin).* From Myoshin-ji. Wood with traces of lacquer. Japan, Kamakura Period, datable to ca. 1286. H. 91.4 cm. 70.67

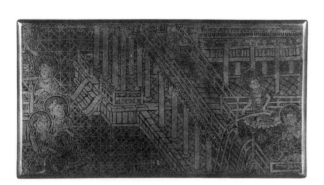

371

*Tabernacle.* Lacquered wood with paintings in color and gold on the interior. Japan, Fujiwara Period, 12th century. H. 160 cm. 69.130

*Box with Chrysanthemum Design.* Lacquer on wood. Japan, Kamakura Period, 1185-1333. W. 27.3 63.513

*Kannon.* Wood with cut gold leaf decoration and polychromy. Japan, Kamakura Period, 13th century. H. 76.2 cm. 52.90

*Amida, Buddha of the Western Paradise.* Dated 1269. Wood, cut gold leaf and polychromy. Koshun and Assistants, Japanese, Kamakura Period. H. 94.6 cm. 60.197

*Wind God.* Wood with traces of polychromy. Japan, Kamakura Period, 13th century. H. 67.3 cm. 72.64

*Head of Ni-o* (one of a pair). Wood. Japan, Kamakura Period, ca. 13th century. H. 75 cm. 70.5

*Zao Gongen.* Wood. Japan, Kamakura Period, 13th century. H. 106.7 cm. 73.105

*Eleven-Headed Kannon.* Hanging scroll, ink, color, and cut gold on silk. Japan, late Fujiwara or early Kamakura Period, late 12th century. H. 106.7 cm. 70.79

*"Monju with the Five Chignons" Riding on a Lion.* Hanging scroll, ink and color on silk. Japan, Kamakura Period, 1185-1333. H. 122 cm. 71.21

*White-Robed Kannon.* From Kozan-ji, Kyoto. Hanging scroll, ink on paper. Japan, Kamakura Period, ca. 1200. H. 91.5 cm. 51.540

*Gohimitsu Bosatsu: The "Secret Five" Bodhisattva.*
Hanging scroll, color, gold, and silver on three joined
pieces of silk. Japan, Kamakura Period, late 12th
century. H. 79 cm. 61.423

*The Poet Taira no Kanemori* (died 990). Section of a
handscroll mounted as a hanging scroll, ink, white, and
slight color on paper. Japan, Kamakura Period,
1185-1333. W. 46.7 cm. 51.397

*Yakushi and the Twelve Generals.*
Hanging scroll mounted on a panel,
ink and color on silk. Japan,
Kamakura Period, 1185-1333.
H. 150.2 cm. 38.422

*Kumano Mandala: The Three Sacred
Shrines.* Hanging scroll, ink and
color on silk. Japan, Kamakura
Period, ca. 1300. H. 134 cm. 53.16

374

*Fukutomi Zoshi* (detail). Handscroll, ink and color on paper. Japan, Kamakura Period, 14th century. W. 10 m. 28.8 cm. 53.358

*One of the "Ten Fast Bulls."* Section of a handscroll mounted as a hanging scroll, ink and slight color on paper. Japan, Kamakura Period, mid-13th century. W. 32.1 cm. 52.286

*Nika Byakudo: The White Path to the Western Paradise Across Two Rivers.* Hanging scroll, ink and color on silk. Japan, Kamakura Period, 13th-14th century. H. 123.5 cm. 55.44

*Yuzu Nembutsu Engi: Efficacy of Repeated Invocations to the Amida Buddha* (detail). Handscroll, ink, color and gold on paper. Japan, Kamakura Period, 14th century. W. 12 m. 87.4 cm. 56.87

*Plum Blossoms.* Hanging scroll, ink on paper. Japan, Nambokucho Period, 1333-1392. H. 103.5 cm. 70.75

*Noh Mask of Ko-beshimi (Small Demon).* Wood with metal insets and polychromy. Japan, Muromachi Period, 1392-1573. H. 20.4 cm. 72.70

*Choyo, Priest Sewing Under the Morning Sun.* Hanging scroll, ink on paper. Kao, Japanese, ca. 1350, Nambokucho Period. H. 83.7 cm. 62.163

*Kasuga Mandala.* Hanging scroll, ink and color on silk. Japan, Nambokucho Period, 1333-1392. H. 119.3 cm. 17.93

*Haboku Landscape.* Hanging scroll, ink on paper. Sesshu, Japanese, 1420-1506, Muromachi Period. H. 71.9 cm. 55.43

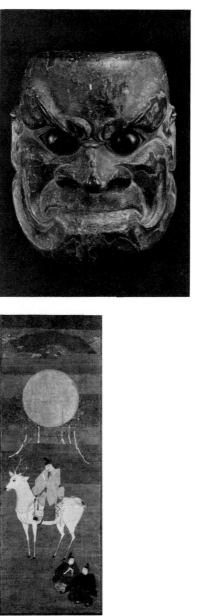

*Landscapes of the Four Seasons.* One of a pair of six-fold screens, ink and
slight color on paper. Ri Shubun, Japanese, active ca. 1424, Muromachi
Period. H. 92.7 cm. 76.93

*Haboku Landscape.* Hanging scroll,
ink on paper. Shugetsu, Japanese,
died ca. 1510, Muromachi Period.
H. 59.6 cm. 76.59

*Winter and Spring Landscape.* Six-fold screen, ink and slight color on paper.
Attributed to Shubun (priest of Shokoku-ji, Kyoto), Japanese, ca. 1414-1463,
Muromachi Period. W. 265.8 cm. 58.476

*Eight Views in the Region of the Hsiao and Hsiang Rivers. Fusuma* panel remounted as a hanging scroll, ink on paper. Ca. 1509. Soami, Japanese, 1485(?)-1525, Muromachi Period. H. 128.6 cm. 63.262

*Horses and Grooms in the Stable* (detail). One of a pair of six-fold screens, ink and color on paper. Japan, Muromachi Period, 1392-1573. W. 348.6 cm. 34.373

*Tiger* and *Dragon.* Pair of six-fold screens, ink on paper. Sesson, Japanese, ca. 1504-ca. 1589, Muromachi Period. W. 339 cm. 59.136, 59.137

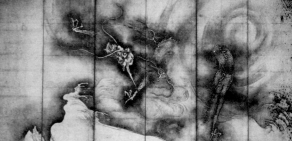

*Namban Byobu: Screen of Southern Barbarians.* One of a pair of six-fold
screens, ink, color, and gold on paper. Japan, Momoyama Period,
ca. 1610-1614. W. 334.3 cm. 60.194

*Bamboo in Wind.* One of a pair of
hanging scrolls, ink on silk. Genga,
Japanese, early 16th century,
Muromachi Period. H. 95.2 cm. 75.71

*Flowers and Birds in a Spring Land-
scape. Fusuma* panel remounted as a
hanging scroll, ink and color on
paper. Attributed to Kano Motonobu,
Japanese, 1476-1559. H. 177.3 cm. 70.6

*Writing Box.* Lacquer on wood with
*maki-e* design. Japan, Muromachi
Period, 15th century. W. 24.2 cm.
69.124

379

*Cosmetic Box.* Lacquer on wood.
Japan, Momoyama Period, 1573-1615.
W. 33.3 cm.  66.25

*Table.* Lacquer on wood with *maki-e* design. Japan,
Muromachi Period, 15th century. W. 58.4 cm.  58.429

*Ewer with Tortoise-Shell Motif.*
Oribe ware, stoneware. Japan,
Momoyama Period, 1573-1615.
H. 21 cm.  58.336

*Water Pot.* Shino ware, stoneware.
Japan, Momoyama Period, 16th
century. H. 18.4 cm.  72.9

*Bowl with Christian Design of Cross and Insignia of the Society of Jesus.* Hagi ware, stoneware. Japan, Momoyama Period, ca. 1600. D. 31 cm. 62.211

*Jar.* Shigaraki ware, stoneware. Japan, Momoyama Period, 1573-1615. H. 28.6 cm. 69.227

*Dish with Design of Valerian and Rocks in a Garden. Nezumi* Shino ware, stoneware. Japan, Momoyama Period, ca. 1610. W. 23.4 cm. 66.24

*Crossing at Sano: Sano no Watari.* Single-panel screen, ink, color, and gold on paper. Nonomura Sotatsu, Japanese, 1576-1643(?), Edo Period. H. 126 cm. 49.554

381

*Dish with Design of Three Wild Geese in Flight. Nezumi* Shino ware, stoneware. Japan, Momoyama Period, ca. 1600. D. 16.5 cm. 59.35

*Chrysanthemums by a Stream.* One of a pair of six-fold screens, ink and color on gold ground paper. Ogata Korin, Japanese, 1658-1716, Edo Period. W. 369.9 cm. 58.207

*Tsuta-no-hosomichi: The Ivy Lane,* section IX from *Ise Monogatari.* Six-fold screen, ink and color on gold ground paper. Fukae Roshu, Japanese, 1699-1757, Edo Period. W. 267.8 cm. 54.127

382

*The Beach at Sumiyoshi,* from *Ise Monogatari (Tales of Ise).* Album leaf, color and gold on paper. Nonomura Sotatsu, Japanese, 1576-1643 (?), Edo Period. H. 24.5 cm.  51.398

*Irises.* One of a pair of six-fold screens, ink and color on gold ground paper. Watanabe Shiko, Japanese, 1683-1755, Edo Period. W. 334.3 cm.  54.604

*Sanjuroku-kasen: The Thirty-Six Immortal Poets.* Two-fold screen, ink and color on paper. Attributed to Kakei (Kagei), active ca. 1740-1750, Edo Period. W. 182.6 cm.  60.183

*The Zen Priest Choka.* Hanging scroll, ink on paper. Nonomura Sotatsu, Japanese, 1576-1643(?), Edo Period. H. 95.8 cm.  58.289

383

*Lions.* One of a pair of six-fold screens, ink and color on gold ground
paper. Yamaguchi Sekkei, Japanese, 1644-1732, Edo Period. W. 333 cm. 72.10

*Poem Scroll* (detail). Handscroll, ink and color on silk
over gold ground paper. Calligraphy by Hon'ami Koetsu,
1558-1637; painting by Nonomura Sotatsu, 1576-1643 (?),
Japanese, Edo Period. W. 543.4 cm. 72.67

*Paulownias and Chrysanthemums.* Two-fold screen, ink,
color, and gold on paper. Sakai Hoitsu, Japanese,
1761-1828, Edo Period. W. 154.9 cm. 64.386

*Flowers of Four Seasons.* One of a pair of six-fold screens, ink and color on paper. Kitagawa Sosetsu, Japanese, active mid-17th century, Edo Period. W. 330.7 cm.  68.193

*The Actor Sanjo Kantaro.* Ink and color on paper. Kaigetsudo Ando, Japanese, Edo Period, ca. 1714. H. 107.5 cm.  61.41

*Bamboo Cliffs After Rain.* Two-fold screen, ink on paper. Ikeno Taiga, Japanese, 1723-1776, Edo Period. W. 182.3 cm.  58.337

*Portrait of the Chinese Priest Dokuritsu.* Dated 1671. Hanging scroll, ink and color on paper. Kita Genki, Japanese, fl. 1664-1698. H. 111.5 cm.  65.31

385

*Gathering at the Orchid Pavilion.* Six-fold screen, ink and slight color on paper. Maruyama Okyo, Japanese, 1733-1795, Edo Period. W. 191.8 cm. 77.1

*Summer Night.* One of a pair of six-fold screens, ink, gold, and silver on paper. Maruyama Okyo, Japanese, 1733-1795, Edo Period. W. 362 cm. 73.157

*Forbidden to the Vulgar.* Hanging scroll, ink on paper. Uragami Gyokudo, Japanese, 1745-1820, Edo Period. H. 134.6 cm. 64.367

*Water Buffalo Returning Home.* Dated 1781. Yosa Buson, Japanese, 1716-1783, Edo Period. H. 130.8 cm. 70.77

*Puppies, Sparrows, and Chrysanthemums.* One of four *fusuma* panels mounted as hanging scrolls, ink and light color on paper. Nagasawa Rosetsu, Japanese, 1754-1799. H. 167.6 cm. 70.71

386

*Inchu-hatsen-zu: The Eight Immortals of Drinking.* One of a pair of six-fold screens, ink and gold on paper. Soga Shohaku, Japanese, 1730-1781, Edo Period. W. 352.4 cm. 76.11

*Horse Race at the Kamo Shrine.* One of a pair of six-fold screens, ink and color on gold ground paper. Japan, Edo Period, 17th century. W. 362 cm. 76.96

*White Prunus.* Dated 1834. Hanging scroll, ink on silk. Yamamoto Baiitsu, Japanese, 1783-1856, Edo Period. H. 172.4 cm. 75.93

*Noh Robe.* Silk embroidery on silk ground overlaid with (beaten) gold leaf. Japan, early 17th century. L. 158.5 cm. 74.36

*Standing Figure of a Beauty.*
Kakiemon-type ware, porcelain. Japan,
Edo Period, late 17th century.
H. 38 cm. 64.366

*Plate with Bird and Flowers.* Kutani
ware, porcelain. Japan, Edo Period,
17th century. D. 29.8 cm. 60.174

*Bowl* (one of a pair). Kakiemon ware,
porcelain. Japan, Edo Period, late
17th century. D. 35.5 cm. 64.364

*Dish with Design of Plovers over
Waves.* Glazed earthenware. Design by
Ogata Korin, 1658-1716; dish by
Ogata Kenzan, 1663-1743, Japanese,
Edo Period. W. 22 cm. 66.365

*Covered Bowl with Chrysanthemums and
Chidori.* Kakiemon ware, porcelain
decorated in colored enamels. Japan,
Edo Period, early 18th century.
D. 21 cm. 61.42

*The Inconstant Type,* from the series *Studies in Physiognomy: Ten Kinds of Women.* Color woodblock prints. Kitagawa Utamaro, Japanese, 1753-1806, Edo Period, Ukiyo-e School. H. 36.2 cm. 30.218

*Fuji in Clear Weather.* Color woodblock print. Katsushika Hokusai, Japanese, 1760-1849, Edo Period, Ukiyo-e School. W. 37.5 cm. 30.189

*The Hurricane,* from the series *Fifty-Three Stations of the Tokaido.* Color woodblock print. Utagawa Hiroshige, Japanese, 1797-1858, Edo Period, Ukiyo-e School. W. 38 cm. 48.307

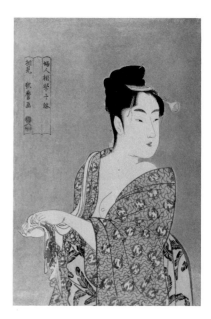

*Matsumoto Koshiro IV as Gorobei, the Fishmonger of Sanya.* Color woodblock print. Sharaku, Japanese, active 1794-1795, Edo Period, Ukiyo-e School. H. 38.5 cm. 74.78

*Youth Representing Monju, God of Wisdom, on a Lion.* Color woodblock print. Suzuki Harunobu, Japanese, 1724-1770, Edo Period, Ukiyo-e School. H. 29.2 cm. 30.177

*Notes*

# Ancient Art of the Americas

*Jadeite Seated Figure.* Mexico, Olmec, before 300. H. 11 cm.  41.390

*Stone Seated Figure.* Mexico, Olmec, before 300. H. 26 cm.  51.179

*Jade Mask.* Mexico, Olmec, before 300. H. 13.7 cm.  67.154

*Stone Ceremonial Axe.* Mexico, Olmec, before 300. H. 32.1 cm.  54.856

*Stone Head.* Mexico, Olmec, 1st-5th century. H. 16.5 cm.  53.369

393

*Jadeite Head.* Mexico, Olmec, 1st-5th century. H. 7.3 cm.  61.31

*Terra-cotta Head.* Mexico, Classic Veracruz Style (Totonac or Tajin), 5th-9th century. H. 28.7 cm.  40.11

*Stone Recumbent Anthropomorphic Figure.* Mexico, Classic Veracruz Style (Totonac or Tajin), 4th-5th century (?). L. 42.1 cm.  48.355

*Terra-cotta Painted Head.* Mexico, Classic Veracruz Style (Totonac or Tajin), 5th-9th century. H. 17.2 cm.  47.26

*Earthenware Seated Figure.* Mexico, Oaxaca, Monte Alban II (Zapotec), 5th-6th century. H. 32.2 cm. 54.857

*Earthenware Dog.* Mexico, Colima, 4th-7th century. H. 39.7 cm. 64.37

*Palma Stone.* Gray volcanic stone. Mexico, Classic Veracruz Style (Totonac or Tajin), ca. 1200. H. 49.2 cm. 73.3

*Yoke.* Serpentine with traces of cinnabar. Mexico, Classic Veracruz Style (Totonac or Tajin), ca. 1000. H. 42.5 cm. 73.213

395

*Gold Shell with Bells.* Mexico,
Oaxaca, Mixtec, after 1000. H. 7.7 cm.
52.86

*Seated Figure of Tlaloc, The Rain God.*
Serpentine. Mexico, Aztec, 13th-15th
century. H. 28.6 cm.  66.361

*Mask.* Turquoise mosaic and terra
cotta. Mexico (?), ca. 1220.
H. 13.8 cm.  67.141

*Monkey.* Stone. Mexico, Tacubaya,
Aztec, 15th century. H. 24.5 cm.
59.125

*Xochipilli, God of Flowers, Dances
and Games.* Stone. Mexico, Aztec,
15th century. H. 27.6 cm.  49.555

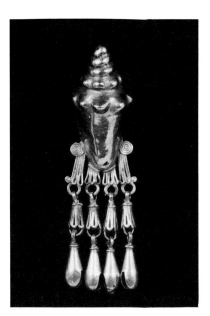

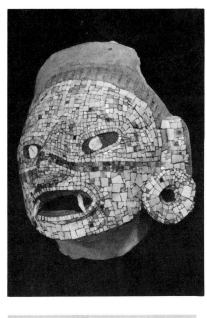

396

*Seated Figure.* Incised shell.
Guatemala, Maya, 3rd-5th century.
H. 16.5 cm. 65.550

*Woman in Ceremonial Robes.* Limestone relief. Mexico
or Guatemala, Usumacinta Region, Maya, ca. 795.
H. 60.3 cm. 62.32

*Stone Head.* Honduras, Copan, Maya,
7th-8th century. H. 52.7 cm.
53.154

*Relief: Part of a Stele.* Limestone.
Mexico or Central America, Maya,
7th-8th century. H. approx.
244.3 cm. 67.29

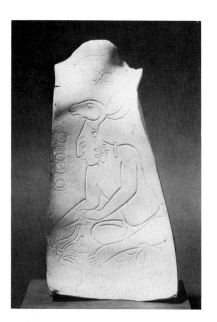

*Incense Burner.* Terra cotta. Mexico, Palenque Region, Maya, 7th-8th century. H. 104.1 cm. 65.248

*Vase.* Earthenware with painted decorations. Guatemala, Kixpec, Maya, 8th-10 century. H. 16.5 cm. 54.391

*Figure of a Warrior.* Terra cotta. Mexico, Yucatan, Island of Guaymil, Maya, 9th-10th century. H. 26.1 cm. 63.93

Left: *Jade Head.* Honduras, Copan, Maya, 7th-8th century. H. 7.6 cm. 47.176. Center: *Jadeite Pendant.* Mexico or Central America, Maya, 6th-8th century. H. 6.8 cm. 52.119 Right: *Plaque.* Crystalline green stone. Mexico or Central America, Maya, 7th-9th century. H. 4.8 cm. 50.153

*Eccentric Flint in Human Shape.*
Stone. Guatemala, Quiriqua, Maya,
6th-8th century. H. 34.6 cm.
50.161

*Jaguar Macehead.* Stone. Costa Rica,
Nicoya, Chorotegan, 8th-9th century.
H. 8.7 cm.  46.469

*Gold Plaque.* Panama, Coclé, 14th-
15th century. H. 25.6 cm.  52.459

*Bird (Head of a Staff).* Gold.
Colombia, Quimbaya, 14th-15th
century. H. 7.5 cm.  54.594

*Gold Pin.* Colombia, Quimbaya, 14th-
15th century. H. 22.7 cm.  47.30

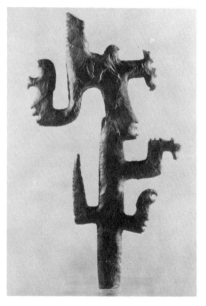

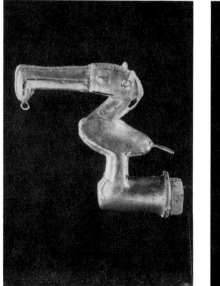

*Double Puma Staff Head.* Gold.
Colombia, Quimbaya, 14th-15th
century. H. 22.7 cm. 44.319

*Anthropomorphic Seated Figure.* Gold.
Colombia, Quimbaya, 14th-15th
century. H. 7.3 cm. 39.509

*Stirrup Jar.* Earthenware. Peru,
Chavin, 1st millennium BC.
H. 22.7 cm. 68.192

*Gold Spoon.* Peru, North Coast,
Chavin, 1st millennium BC.
L. 17.5 cm. 58.177

*Gold Plaque.* Peru, North Coast,
Chavin, 1st millennium BC.
H. 21.8 cm. 46.117

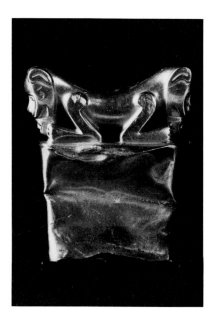

400

*Bowl with Incised Decoration.* Stone.
Peru, North Coast, Chavin, 1st
millennium BC. H. 6.5 cm. 55.167

*Finial in the Form of a Monkey.*
Gold. Peru, North Coast, Mochica,
1st-5th century. H. 36.8 cm.
49.197

*Border of a Mantle.* Painted cotton tabby. Peru, South Coast, Paracas,
Early Period. Over-all: W. 254.2 cm. Detail: W. 68.5 cm. 40.530

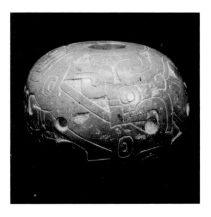

*Poncho.* Needle *réseau,* wool. Peru, South Coast, Paracas, Early Period. H. 94 cm.  40.514

*Part of a Mantle.* Embroidery, wool. Peru, South Coast, Paracas, Early Period. Over-all: W. 139 cm. Detail: H. 47 cm.  40.528

*Fringed Poncho.* Embroidery, wool. Peru, South Coast, Paracas, Early Period. H. 147.5 cm.  46.227

*Mosaic Relief.* Peru, North (?) Coast, Tiahuanaco, 9th-10th century. H. 6.5 cm.  44.291

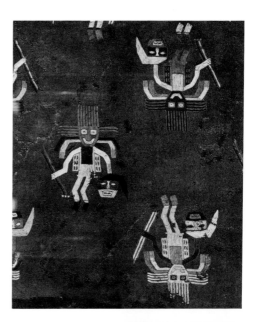

402

*Textile.* Tapestry weave, wool and cotton. Peru, South Coast, Tiahuanaco, Middle Period. H. 39.4 cm. 57.495

*Poncho.* Tapestry weave, wool and cotton. Peru, South Coast, Tiahuanaco, Middle Period. W. 115 cm. 56.84

*Jar.* Earthenware with painted decoration. Peru, South Coast, Tiahuanaco, 10th-12th century. H. 36.7 cm. 55.173

*Square Hat.* Knotted pile, wool. Peru, South Coast, Tiahuanaco, Middle Period. H. 14.3 cm. 45.378

*Front of a Litter.* Painted wood. Peru, North Coast, Chimu, 12th-13th century. H. 57.8 cm.  52.233

*Poncho.* Tapestry weave, wool and cotton. Peru, South Coast, Inca Culture, 1400-1532. H. 85 cm. 57.136

*Half Poncho.* Tapestry weave, wool and cotton. Peru, Inca Period, 16th century. H. 95.3 cm.  51.393

*Notes*

# North American Indian Art

406

*Ladle.* Carved horn and bone.
Northwest Coast, Tlingit. L. 30.5 cm.
53.386

*Bowl.* Earthenware. United States,
New Mexico, Mimbres Valley, ca.
1000-1200. D. 20.5 cm. 73.165

*Breastplate.* Quill and feathers.
United States, Northern Plains,
late 19th century. H. 44.5 cm.
37.859

*Covered Basket.* United States,
Oregon, Klamath River, Yurok Tribe.
H. 18.4 cm. 17.498

*Necklace.* Silver. United States,
Arizona, Navajo, ca. 1900.
L. 39.3 cm. 16.173

*Bowl Basket.* United States.
California, Panamint Tribe.
D. 43.2 cm. 17.499

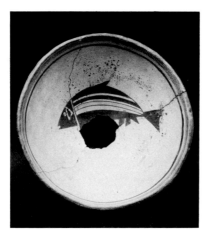

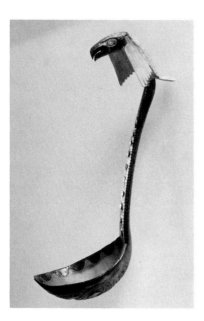

*Jar.* Earthenware. United States, New Mexico, Zuni
Pueblo. H. 26 cm. 23.1082

*Plate.* Earthenware. Maria Martinez
and Po Povida, 1968, United States,
New Mexico, San Ildefonso Pueblo,
D. 26.4 cm. 70.508

*Ceremonial Blanket.* Mountain-goat wool, cedar bark.
Northwest Coast, Tlingit, late 19th century. W. 162.5 cm.
55.614

*Woman's Dress.* Leather and beads. United States,
Sioux, late 19th century. L. 142.3 cm. 32.44

*Notes*

African Art

*Mule's Head.* Wood and metal. Africa, Mali, Bambara Tribe (Bamana), before 1935. H. 40.7 cm. 35.307

*Mask with Female Figure (Satimbe?).* Wood. Africa, Mali, Sanga (?), Dogon Tribe, probably ca. 1940. H. 111.2 cm. 60.169

*Snake.* Painted wood. Africa, Guinea, Baga Tribe, Landuman Subtribe (?), before 1958. H. 148 cm. 60.37

*Woman and Child (ancestor or maternity group?).* Wood. Africa, Ivory Coast, Korhogo District, Senufo Tribe (Siena), probably ca. 1930. H. 63.5 cm. 61.198

*Miniature Mask.* Cast gold. Africa, Ivory Coast, Baule Tribe, before 1951. H. 7.5 cm. 54.602

*Seated Figure.* Soapstone. Africa, Guinea, Kisi River Area, 18th century (?). H. 23.8 cm. 76.29

*Plaque with Warrior.* Bronze.
Africa, Nigeria, Benin City,
17th century. H. 49.4 cm.
53.425

*Altar Portrait of a Deceased Oba.*
Bronze. Africa, Nigeria, Benin City,
17th century. H. 29.9 cm.  38.6

*Post Sculpture with Two Figures.*
Painted wood. Africa, Nigeria,
Yoruba Tribe, ca. 1920. H. 106.7
H. 106.7 cm.  69.55

*Bush Cow Mask.* Painted wood.
Africa, Upper Volta, Bobo-Diulasso
District, probably ca. 1940-1950.
H. 69.8 cm.  69.2

*One of a Pair of Lions.* Wood. Africa, Dahomey, Baname
Village, Donvidé Family, ca. 1940. H. 35.9 cm.  65.324

*Helmet Mask.* Wood. Africa, Cameroon Grasslands, Bamum Tribe, ca. 1900. H. 57.2 cm. 67.151

*Mask.* Wood and fiber. Africa, Kwango-Kwilu Area, Zaïre, Bayaka Tribe, ca. 1935-1940. H. 47 cm. 69.8

*Helmet Mask.* Painted wood. Africa, Kasai-Sankuru Area, Zaïre, Bakuba Tribe, probably late 19th century. H. 43.2 cm. 35.304

*Ancestor Figure.* Wood. Africa, Upper Lualaba Area, Zaïre, Basikasingo Tribe, probably before 1930. H. 48.2 cm. 69.10

*Male Cult Figure.* Wood. Africa, Kwango-Kwilu Area, Zaïre, Bayaka Tribe, probably ca. 1900. H. 61 cm. 70.34

*Standing Male Figure.* Wood, iron, and glass. Africa, Congo-Brazzaville, Bakongo Tribe or Bavili Sub-Tribe, early 19th century. H. 55.9 cm. 74.186

# Notes

# Oceanic Art

*Kamanggabi Figure.* Painted wood and cowrie shell. Melanesia, New Guinea, Central Sepik River District, Arambak People, probably ca. 1920-1930, H. 207 cm.  63.553

*Ancestral Figure.* Painted wood with fiber and tapa cloth. Melanesia, New Guinea, Middle Sepik River, 19th century. H. 105.4 cm.  71.150

*Suspension Hook.* Painted wood. Melanesia, New Guinea, Sepik River, ca. 1940 (?). H. 56.5 cm.  70.21

*Canoe Splashboard.* Wood. Melanesia, New Guinea, Massim Area, Trobriand Islands, 19th century. H. 58.7 cm. 66.130

*War Shield.* Painted wood. Melanesia, Dutch New Guinea, Asmat, ca. 1940. H. 176.5 cm.  63.554

*Lintel.* Wood. Polynesia, New Zealand, Maori, early 19th century.
H. 35 cm. 62.350

*Stilt Footrest.* Wood. Polynesia,
Marquesas Islands, early 19th century.
H. 38.1 cm. 70.114

*Staff (U'u).* Stained ironwood.
Polynesia, Marquesas Islands, early
19th century. H. 148.3 cm.
63.255

*Ceremonial Adze.* Wood, stone and
fiber. Polynesia, Central Hervey
Islands, probably late 19th century.
H. 124.5 cm. 40.1078

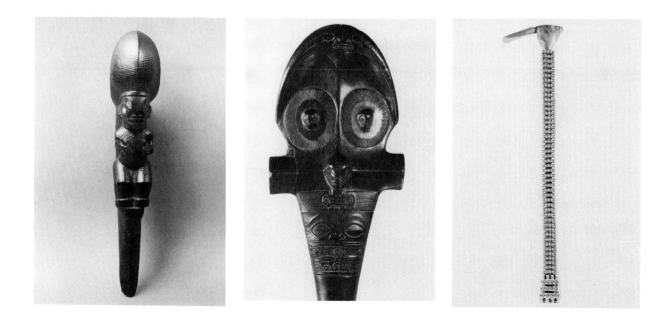

418

*Malanggan Memorial Festival Pole.*
Painted wood, sea snail opercula.
Melanesia, New Ireland, 19th
century. H. 92.7 cm. 71.149

*Yoke.* Wood. Polynesia, Easter Islands, 19th century. L. 69.8 cm. 61.406

*Notes*

# Artist Index

*Only individual artists are included in this index. Consult the table of contents for works with period or school attributions.*